WHY DO THE NATIONS RAGE?

WHY DO THE NATIONS RAGE?

The Demonic Origin Of Nationalism

DAVID A. RITCHIE

Foreword by Yancey C. Arrington

WIPF & STOCK · Eugene, Oregon

WHY DO THE NATIONS RAGE?
The Demonic Origin of Nationalism

Wipf & Stock
An Imprint of Wipf and Stock Publishers
199 W. 8th Ave., Suite 3
Eugene, OR 97401

www.wipfandstock.com

PAPERBACK ISBN: 978-1-6667-3220-7
HARDCOVER ISBN: 978-1-6667-2561-2
EBOOK ISBN: 978-1-6667-2562-9

DECEMBER 28, 2021 8:38 AM

To Kate Ritchie,
my beloved, my bride, my best friend, my helpmate

Contents

LIST OF ILLUSTRATIONS

FOREWORD

by Yancey C. Arrington

On January 6, 2021, the images of men and women riotously barreling their way into the United States Capitol building shocked not only the nation but the global community at large. We witnessed windows smashed, chamber doors barricaded, and even lives lost. The scenes were both surreal and terrifying. I was especially concerned knowing that my brother, a U.S. Congressman, was in the House Chambers behind those barricaded doors.

The last time the Capitol was stormed was in 1814. The culprits of that bygone event were British soldiers who, at the time, were engaged in a war with the United States. However, those who stormed the American citadel in 2021 were in fact its own citizens. Americans from around the country, armed with political banners, signs, and flags bearing messages and maxims of the far right, were engaged in a conflict of their own. Believing the propaganda that the election of the newest U.S. President was somehow illegitimate, these individuals wanted to violently take civic measures into their own hands. Consequently, democracy-loving countries around the world watched in horror as they saw Americans siege their own capitol. It was a political tragedy of historic proportions.

But it wasn't the only tragedy. There was another calamity playing itself out. Peppered throughout the riotous masses were also Christian images and rhetoric: crosses held aloft, placards with religious statements like "Jesus Saves," and Christian flags flying alongside American ones. To many of the participants, the

Capitol Riot was more than a political activity, it was a spiritual one—in fact, an explicitly Christian one. In their thinking, the United States is God's modern-day corollary to ancient Israel. America should be seen as being anointed with a messianic identity. That day on the Capitol was the coming out party of Christian nationalism.

Adherents promote the notion that the United States is a country founded by faith for faith, with America's faith being a specific brand of conservative evangelicalism. Additionally, whatever political affiliations, perspectives, and positions that tie themselves to this vein of conservative evangelicalism often become idolized as the essence of America herself. Thus, while statements that conflate the relationship between church and state such as "Jesus is my Savior and Trump is my President" or "The G.O.P. is God's Own Party" might make many Republican Christians recoil, they sound perfectly acceptable to Christian nationalists.

I should know. I, like the author, was raised in West Texas where Christian nationalism was the predominant point of view. Growing up I was indirectly taught by my community (e.g., school, church, home) that there was only one political party to join, only one set of views to hold, and only one way to run a democracy. Those who offered different perspectives weren't only wrong, they were unpatriotic; they were somehow less American. Moreover, they were immoral and spiritually counterfeit of any Christian faith they claimed to possess. This was the pernicious dogma of Christian nationalism of my youth.

Unfortunately, with the help of the church, that same spirit from my younger days has endured and established itself in far more places around the United States. A fact that was undoubtedly on full display in HD on televisions sets around the world that fateful January day. Shockingly, I discovered that some of my own congregants had attended, in full support of what transpired. It reminded me that Christian nationalism isn't a West Texas phenomenon but an American one. Yet with that said, at the writing of this foreword, the FBI is charging a family of five for their involvement

in the Capitol Riot. The family's origin? The small town of Borger
. . . in West Texas. Different decade, same spirit.

The pull of Christian nationalism is strong. Believers of every
shade and stripe have been discipled in it. Pastors rally their congregations around it. Churches split over it.

What are we to do?

The irony for Christian nationalists is that while they are correct in believing the problems at hand in America are really spiritual in nature, they are blind to the fact that those same spiritual
compromises actually lie in them. Indeed, the primary locus of the
Christian struggle is in the church not the state. It's found in the
hearts of well-meaning believers who, to use Augustine's framework, conflate the kingdom of God with the kingdom of man.
It's understanding that the church isn't apolitical but alternatively
political, where our ultimate allegiance is to a King and a kingdom
whose symbol is a cross not a capitol. This cruciform kingdom
teaches us that much of what is good, true, and beautiful isn't accomplished by worldly power and political maneuvering but with
gospel intentionality, sacrificial service, and loving our neighbor
while we sojourn in this world looking toward the arrival of the
new world without end. This is the banner under which followers
of Jesus stand.

And as David A. Ritchie will demonstrate in his important
work *Why Do the Nations Rage*, those given to Christ must realize
there is also more at play in nationalism than what meets the eye.
It is something ancient and sinister, an evil our biblical forebears
faced centuries ago.

David will help us see that the contest the church has with
nationalism is actually one of spiritual warfare. It is a struggle
against principalities and powers—a battle with the demonic—
where our only hope and recourse is the glory and goodness of the
gospel. This is the solution to which David will point us. And if we
humble ourselves, read thoughtfully, and reflect deeply upon his
words, may the Lord, in his grace, use *Why Do the Nations Rage*
to help deliver a generation of Christians from the abyss of what
ultimately is a false religion.

Those are the kind of stakes tied to this work.
For the glory of God and the goodness of the gospel,
For the integrity of the church and her witness to the world,
For the sake of your own soul,

Read and read well.

Dr. Yancey C. Arrington
Teaching Pastor, Clear Creek Community Church
Houston, Texas
July 2021

Acknowledgements

A DECADE AGO, I do not believe I would have listed nationalism among the great threats to the people of God. Now, I would argue that it is one of the most significant false gospels that seeks to oppose and infiltrate the church. Pastoral ministry has allowed me to see nationalism as a spiritual danger. Theology has given me the language and the categories to understand and communicate why it is so dangerous.

This project is, thus, indebted to the people of Redeemer Christian Church in Amarillo, Texas. Thank you for allowing me to be your pastor, as we seek to stumble toward Jesus together. I am especially grateful for Redeemer's elders, deacons, and staff members, with whom I co-labor alongside for the sake of the gospel. What a joy it is to serve God and his people with you!

I want to express my sincerest gratitude to Dr. Paul S. Jeon, of Reformed Theological Seminary in Washington D.C., for his time, wisdom, and practical advice in writing this project. Without his encouragement, support, and advocation, this project would have never become a published book. Thank you to Ramona Coffman, Joshua Morrow, Christopher Myers, Bryan Padgett, Remoy Philip, Seth Wieck, Dr. Joshua Heavin, Dr. Milton Jones, and Dr. Samuel L. Perry for their extensive feedback and critiques of an early manuscript. Thank you to my editor Matthew Wimer and the team at Wipf and Stock Publishers for granting me the opportunity to publish my first book. Thank you to my publicist Blake I. Collier. Thank you to Dr. Yancey C. Arrington for graciously writing the foreword to this work. Thank you to Julie and Steve Ritchie, my mom and dad, who have faithfully loved, supported, and cheered me on in the trials and tribulations of life and ministry. Thank you to my sons Solomon, Samuel, and Simon Peter Ritchie, for being my best little buddies—it is a joy to be your father, and I love you more than words can say.

Lastly, thank you to Kate Ritchie; my brilliant and beautiful wife, my very best friend in the world. Thank you for encouraging me to write about this topic, and thank you for being my very favorite conversation partner for ministry, theology, and pretty much everything else in life. We did this together. Many women have done excellently, but you surpass them all (Prov 31:29).

Rev. David A. Ritchie
Lead Pastor, Redeemer Christian Church
Amarillo, Texas
October 2021

List of Abbreviations

HEBREW BIBLE/OLD TESTAMENT

Gen
Exod
Lev
Deut
Josh
Judg
Ruth
1–2 Sam
1–2 Kgs
1–2 Chr
Ps (*pl.* Pss)
Prov
Isa
Jer
Ezek
Dan
Mic

NEW TESTAMENT

Matt
Mark
Luke

John
Acts
Rom
1–2 Cor
Gal
Eph
Phil
Col
1–2 Tim
Heb
1–2 Pet
1–2–3 John
Rev

APOCRYPHAL/DEUTEROCANONICAL BOOKS AND OTHER ANCIENT SOURCES

Sir   Ben Sirach/Ecclesiasticus
Jub   Jubilees
DSS   The Dead Sea Scrolls
LXX   The Septuagint (the ancient Greek Old Testament)

BIBLE TRANSLATIONS

ESV   *The Holy Bible: English Standard Version.* Wheaton, IL: Crossway Bibles, 2016.

LES   Brannan, Rick, Ken M. Penner, Israel Loken, Michael Aubrey, and Isaiah Hoogendyk, eds. *The Lexham English Septuagint.* Bellingham, WA: Lexham, 2012.

KJV   *The Holy Bible: King James Version.* Electronic Edition of the 1900 Authorized Version. Bellingham, WA: Logos, 2009.

NASB   *New American Standard Bible: 1995 Update.* La Habra, CA: The Lockman Foundation, 1995.

NIV   *The New International Version.* Grand Rapids, MI: Zondervan, 2011.

NKJV   *The New King James Version.* Nashville: Thomas Nelson, 1982.

NRSV   *The Holy Bible: New Revised Standard Version.* Nashville: Thomas Nelson 1989.

REFERENCE WORKS

ANET   *Ancient Near East Texts Relating to the Old Testament.* James B. Pritchard. 2nd ed. Princeton: Princeton University Press, 1955.

AYBD   *The Anchor Yale Bible Dictionary.* Edited by David Noel Freedman, Gary A. Herion, David F. Graf, John David Pleins, and Astrid B. Beck. New York: Doubleday, 1992.

BDAG   *A Greek-English Lexicon of the New Testament and Other Early Christian Literature.* Walter Bauer, Frederick W. Danker, William Arndt, and F. Wilbur Gingrich. 3rd ed. Chicago: University of Chicago Press, 2000.

EDB   *Eerdmans Dictionary of the Bible.* Edited by David Noel Freedman, Allen C. Myers, and Astrid B. Beck. Grand Rapids, MI: Eerdmans, 2000.

DDD   *Dictionary of Deities and Demons in the Bible.* Edited by Karel van der Toorn, Bob Becking, and Pieter W. van der Horst, 2nd ed. Grand Rapids: Eerdmans, 1999.

HALOT   *The Hebrew and Aramaic Lexicon of the Old Testament.* Edited by Ludwig Koehler, Walter Baumgartner, M. E. J. Richardson, and Johann Jakob Stamm. Leiden: E.J. Brill, 1994–2000.

ODCC   *The Oxford Dictionary of the Christian Church.* Edited by F. L. Cross and Elizabeth A. Livingstone. Oxford: Oxford University Press, 2005.

LIST OF ABBREVIATIONS

TDNT   *Theological Dictionary of the New Testament.* Edited
          by Gerhard Kittel, Geoffrey W. Bromiley, and Ger-
          hard Friedrich. Grand Rapids, MI: Eerdmans, 1964–.
TLOT   *Theological Lexicon of the Old Testament.* Ernst Jenni
          and Claus Westermann. Peabody, MA: Hendrickson,
          1997.

Part I

More Things in Heaven and Earth

1

A PEOPLE POSSESSED

"A nation is a soul, a spiritual principle."

—ERNEST RENAN, *QU'EST-CE QU'UNE NATION?* (1882)

"See to it that no one takes you captive by philosophy and empty deceit, according to human tradition, according to the elemental spirits of the world, and not according to Christ."

—COLOSSIANS 2:8

A RIVAL RELIGION

The gallows got my attention. They arose from the chaos, signaling murderous intent, as the mob surged like a tsunami around the Capitol steps. "Hang Mike Pence!" voices shouted in unison as realtors and veterans and insurance agents, now insurgents, pressed and burst into the federal building. Lawmakers fled, as men wearing tactical gear swept the legislative chambers with zip-ties in

3

hand, presumably for the purpose of arresting and punishing those leaders deemed treasonous. Some of the rioters came prepared for revolution. Some seem to have been swept up in the spirit of the moment, unaware of the ramifications of what their choices would have on their lives and their nation.

On that day, January 6, 2021, as I saw pictures and footage of the events transpiring in the United States Capitol, I felt angry that the violent political rhetoric in American politics had now increasingly manifested in violent actions. I felt concerned that this extreme event might be a prelude to an even more extreme future. I felt ashamed that such displays had now come to be expected from my nation's toxic political theater. Most of all, as a pastor, I felt grieved that images of the name of my Savior were displayed alongside this spectacle of nihilistic division and death.

In the days that followed, videos surfaced of worship songs being sung on the Capitol lawn during the invasion and of the man with the iconic horned helmet and star-spangled face-paint offering a prayer "in Christ's holy name" within the invaded Senate Chamber. Consequently, think pieces on the topic of "Christian nationalism" began to dominate editorial pages and social media feeds.

How did it come to this? How did Christianity come to be so identified with the ideology known as nationalism? How could some Christians themselves be so enchanted, so deceived, so (dare I say) *possessed* so as to justify conspiracy theories, mob violence, and insurrection?

Despite the recent focus on what many term as "white Christian nationalism" in America, nationalism itself is not inherently bound to any one ethnicity, religion, or nationality.[1] Nor is it by any means a recent phenomenon. In fact, nationalism studies surged as the dust settled from World War 2, as a way to understand, reckon

---

1. Admittedly, the most noxious—and unified—form of nationalism in the contemporary United States is "white Christian nationalism," and there is an avalanche of disheartening sociological data that supports this claim. See: Whitehead and Perry, *Taking America Back for God.* However, I want to stress that white Christian nationalism is only one manifestation of a much broader and deeply historical form of spiritual idolatry.

with, and hopefully prevent the devastation of such global conflict. Interestingly, the same time period saw a corresponding increase in interest regarding the Apostle Paul's doctrine of "powers."[2] In exploring the powers, theologians rediscovered biblical language and categories to describe the spiritual evil that inspired Nazi Germany to inflict the unimaginable horror of the Holocaust.

But what if nationalism and the powers are more than casually related? What if the biblical category of powers actually helps explain the spiritual aspects and agencies behind nationalism in ways that the social sciences could not? What if the Apostle Paul can help us understand why nationalism is such an enduring and alluring form of idolatry, especially among people of faith today?

I have no intention of demeaning or devaluing sociological or historical perspectives on nationalism. Studying nationalism through the familiar lens of the social sciences can yield helpful and indispensable insights.[3] We don't need less than the social sciences. But we do need something more; something that helps us see beyond the confined horizons of the "immanent frame."[4] Indeed, there are more things in heaven and earth than are dreamt of in our secular philosophy, and a biblically-derived spiritual realism brings forth a necessary perspective for Christians to

2. The term "powers" comes from the *KJV* translation of *"exousias"* in Ephesians 6:12, which refer to spiritual forces of darkness, which the *NKJV* and *NASB* still follow. Although other modern English translations prefer to translate *"exousias,"* as "authorities," the spiritual forces described in Ephesians 6:12 are still most often termed "powers" by New Testament biblical scholars and theologians.

3. To the potential consternation of some readers, this book is not primarily an analysis of contemporary Christian nationalism. Rather, this book is intended to function as a biblical-theological critique of the broad phenomenon of nationalism and the spiritual foundations that lie at its core. For sociological critiques of Christian nationalism in the United States, see: Whitehead and Perry, *Taking America Back for God* and Gorski and Perry, *The Flag and the Cross*.

4. By the phrase "immanent frame," I refer to the condition of secularism wherein any notion of transcendent reality is presuppositionally contested. " . . . this frame constitutes a 'natural' order, to be contrasted with a supernatural one, an 'immanent' world over against a possible 'transcendent' one." Taylor, *A Secular Age*, 542.

understand and navigate the transcendent dynamics behind nations and nationalism.

Since nationalism involves the exaltation of a nation (or a particular conception[5] of a nation) to the highest place of allegiance, concern, and devotion, it is essentially idolatrous, as several Christian critics of nationalism have observed. However, in the coming pages, I will argue that nationalism is inherently demonic as well.

Through an interdisciplinary analysis of scholarship on nationalism and Paul's doctrine of powers, we will learn how the impulse behind nationalism is as ancient as the tower of Babel and as demonic as the worship of Baal. Indeed, when examined through the lens of biblical demonology, you will discover that there is little distinction between the ancient pagan's worship of a national patron deity and the contemporary nationalist's tendency to exalt a particular nation to a place of functional divinity.

I will be upfront with my goal. By the time you come the final page of this book, I want you to see that Christianity and nationalism are rival religions.

I write about nationalism, not as an armchair theologian with a political axe to grind. I write about nationalism because my experience as a pastor in the West Texas wilderness has led me to believe that nationalism—not atheism, not new age spiritualism, nor any other traditional world faith—is the greatest religious rival to the Christian gospel that vies for the worship of the people whom I love and serve in my congregation, my broader community, and, increasingly, my nation.

As a rival religion, nationalism may seek to conquer Christianity, or it may seek to co-opt Christianity for its own purposes. To borrow some imagery from the book of Revelation, as a "Beast," nationalism may seek to destroy Christianity through the power

---

5. By "conception," I'm alluding to the fact that there are differing visions as to what a given nation should be and thus different (or variegated) versions of nationalism. Some iterations of nationalism are more ethnically oriented (i.e., black nationalism, white nationalism), some are more ideologically oriented (i.e., Bolshevism, revolutionary France, extremism in modern political parties), and some are a combination of the two (i.e., white Christian nationalism, Nazism). See chapter 3 for more on the variegated nature of nationalism.

of the sword (cf. Rev 13). But as a "Babylon," it may seek to compromise Christianity through the power of seduction (cf. Rev 18).[6] Likewise, the wicked Queen Jezebel sought to ruthlessly destroy all prophets of Yahweh, whereas the false prophet Balaam sought to lead the people of Israel astray through syncretism and idolatry. Yet both Jezebel and Balaam were worshippers of Baal. In exalting the nation to a place of spiritual ultimacy, nationalism effectively turns the nation into an idol of a false god. Christians must flee such idolatry, for to serve or make sacrifices to such idols is to share fellowship with demonic powers who are actively opposed to God and his people (cf. 1 Cor 10:20–21).

A ROADMAP GOING FORWARD

In the remaining chapters of Part I, I will introduce the concepts of "powers," "nations," and "nationalism." After establishing a common framework and vocabulary, we will move toward a biblical-theological critique of nationalism by using Paul's doctrine of powers as the primary lens of analysis. In Part II, we will explore the rich intellectual history that lies behind the powers, primarily deriving from the Hebrew Scriptures as well as a few other ancient sources. This will reveal not only the origin of the powers, but also the deeply ancient connection between the powers and the pagan nations. Part III will unfold how the Apostle Paul understands the powers, the nations, and nationalistic allegiance in light of the redemptive accomplishment of Jesus Christ. Arguably the most significant section of the book, Part IV will show the various ways that nationalism, in all of its myriad forms, consistently conveys its own set of spiritually-charged, religious doctrines that simultaneously mirror and distort the Christian gospel. Finally, Part V will offer a practical sketch for contending with the powers

---

6. Leithart offers the distinction of "beasts" and "babels" to categorize the way that empires have opposed Christianity. I believe this distinction also applies to the way nationalism opposes Christianity. Thus, what is often referred to as "Christian nationalism" is a babel-like variety of nationalism. Leithart, *Between Babel and Beast*, xi.

of nationalism in a ministerial context, along with a final pastoral charge.

2

THE POWERS THAT BE

INTRODUCING THE POWERS

While significant space will be devoted in later chapters to Paul's understanding of powers, a brief introduction to the concept is in order. Simply stated, Paul presents the powers as spiritual beings that are personal in nature and exert corporate influence over groups of people.[1] Although the powers are clearly related to the concept of demons, Paul does not typically employ the term "demons" (*daimonion*) when describing forces of spiritual evil.[2] Instead, he uses the terms "rulers" (*archē*), "authorities" (*exousias*), "powers" (*dynamis*), "dominions" (*kyriotēs*), "thrones" (*thronos*), or "cosmic powers" (*kosmokratōr*) as cognate terms when describing such entities.[3] In utilizing this language, Paul implies that the powers bear negative influence not only over individuals but also people groups and geographical territories.

---

1. See Rom 8:38; 1 Cor 2:8, 15:24–26; Eph 1:20, 2:1, 3:10, 6:12; Col 1:16, 2:26 for key New Testament passages on the powers.

2. Paul does, however, use the term *daimonion* in 1 Cor 10:20–21 and 1 Tim 4:1.

3. Heiser, *Demons,* 220.

Paul's use of powers is also "apocalyptic" in nature.[4] Here, "apocalyptic" carries the notion of that which was once concealed being suddenly, dramatically, and irreversibly revealed or unveiled. When referring to the "rulers," "authorities," and "cosmic powers over this present darkness," Paul is lifting a curtain. He is *unveiling* the true nature of spiritual reality that lies behind the "flesh and blood" of human experience and human history (Eph 6:12). To preclude these powers from how we understand reality is to miss the whole picture and wonder of biblical cosmology. In an unenchanted wasteland of a secular age, we are prone to interpret ourselves, our world, and even Scripture itself within the constraints of mere matter in motion. But within this truncated, cropped-frame view of reality, the Apostle Paul's apocalyptic framework invites use into a "widescreen edition" of the cosmos we inhabit and the unseen spiritual drama that surrounds us.[5]

As biblical scholar J. Louis Martyn observed, Paul's apocalyptic perspective views the drama of salvation not as a two-actor drama, consisting only of God and humanity. Rather, Christian salvation is a three-actor drama consisting of God, humanity, and the cosmic powers.[6] In Christ, God has dramatically—and *apocalyptically*—acted upon the world, which has been under the tyranny of the anti-God powers. The arrival of Christ has inaugurated the age of New Creation that is contrasted with "the present evil age" (Gal 1:4), wherein the peoples of the earth have been under cosmic enslavement.[7]

---

4. In recent years, several scholars have understood the powers to play a prominent role within the *apocalyptic* framework of Paul's letters. These scholars include Ernst Käsemann, J. Louis Martyn, Beverly Roberts Gaventa, and Philip Ziegler. Fleming Rutledge gives a particularly helpful overview of various themes of this "apocalyptic theology" in her chapter titled "The Apocalyptic War" in Rutledge, *Crucifixion*, 353–360.

5. This illustration is adapted from Gaventa, "The Cosmic Power of Sin in Paul's Letter to the Romans," 231.

6. Martyn, "Epilogue: An Essay in Pauline Meta-Ethics." In *Divine and Human Agency in Paul and His Cultural Environment*, 177–178.

7. Martyn, *Galatians*, 97–99.

Nevertheless, in this present age, the powers seek to separate people from the love of God (Rom 8:38). They apparently possessed and controlled the imperial means that crucified Christ (1 Cor 2:8). They blind the minds of unbelievers to the light of the gospel (2 Cor 4:4). They are the beings with whom spiritual war is waged (Eph 6:12). Yet, they have now been defeated and delegitimized by the far greater power of the resurrected and ascended Lord Jesus Christ (Eph 1:20–22).

THE MONSTERS IN THE MACHINE

For many years, the powers were a relatively neglected niche of Pauline studies, especially among Protestants in the West. After the Enlightenment, many theologians had barely enough room for God in their view of reality, let alone angels and demons.[8] Indeed, many contended that for Christianity to have a respectable place in the world (or, more honestly, Western Academia), Christian doctrine would need to be demythologized and redefined. As twentieth-century German theologian Rudolph Bultmann writes, "We cannot use electric lights and radios and, in the event of illness, avail ourselves of modern medicine and clinical means and at the same time believe in the spirit and wonder world of the New Testament."[9]

However, as alluded to in the previous chapter, the horror and atrocities of World War 2 changed the horizons of theological imagination. Demons and devils became not only plausible but, in some sense, undeniable realities. As a result, the powers of Paul began to receive their long-overdue attention. As one scholar remarks, "There are many times and regions where these texts [i.e., the writings of Paul] remain a sealed book. And then suddenly conditions can arise which make it visible that these words have a power to unveil and liberate."[10]

8. Wink, *The Powers That Be*, 23.

9. Bultmann, *New Testament & Mythology*, 4.

10. Berkhof, *Christ and the Powers*, 11.

In the early 1950s, both Hendrik Berkhof and G.B. Caird independently presented lectures on the powers, which were subsequently published as some of the primary, modern resources in protestant theology regarding the subject.[11] In both of these early works, Berkhof and Caird argued that, for Paul, powers refer primarily to oppressive social, political, economic, and religious structures. The powers, in their view, helped describe how corrupt organizations, institutions, and governments not only can propagate an abstract evil culture, they seem to possess an evil *personality*.

A vivid illustration of this concept may be seen in *The Grapes of Wrath*, when author John Steinbeck describes the scene of a farmer in Oklahoma losing his land to foreclosure. Due to drought and dust bowl, and the ensuing years of crop failure, the hardworking man was forced to offer his family's land as collateral to the Bank. But despite the loans for new seed and a new season of planting, the rain does not fall. The crops do not come.

When the owners drive onto the land to demand the tenants to move, they explain that their hands are tied: "The Bank—or the Company—needs—wants—insists—must have—as though the Bank or the Company were a monster, with thought and feeling, which had ensnared them."[12] The bankmen say that the Bank doesn't breathe air or eat side meat. The Bank breathes profits. It eats interest on money, and if it doesn't eat—it dies.

The farmer protests and says, "but the bank is only made of men." But the owner corrects him, "The bank is something else than men. It happens every man in a bank hates what the bank does, and yet the bank does it. The bank is something more than men I tell you. It's the monster. Men made it, but they can't control it."[13]

The powers, thus, take on a transhuman, spiritual quality that animate human structures and communities into monstrous

---

11. See: Berkhof, *Christ and the Powers* and Caird, *Principalities and Powers*.

12. Steinbeck, *The Grapes of Wrath*, 43.

13. Steinbeck, *The Grapes of Wrath*, 45.

entities. The powers perpetuate the fallenness of God's creation and the dehumanization of God's image bearers. They are the why the bankman will begrudgingly expel a starving family from their home and land. They are why the Nazi soldier feels compelled to "just follow his orders" and close the gas chamber door.

BIBLICAL REALISM

The tradition of *powers-as-social-structures* finds its maturation in the theological work of Walter Wink, namely his trilogy on the powers.[14] Within this framework, the powers help name and un-mask the corporate reality of spiritual evil behind social ills such as racism, poverty, and injustice in ways that are specific and tangible. Such a view of the powers is a healthy corrective to the incipient materialism of many liberal theologians and the individualism of their conservative counterparts. However, by conflating the pow-ers exclusively with this-worldly structures, theological thinkers, such as Wink, reveal an ever-present temptation to completely im-manentize and nominalize the powers.

Over against such spiritual nominalism, Ghanaian theolo-gian Esther E. Acolatse argues for a perspective she terms "bibli-cal realism." She observes that a major factor in the theological estrangement between churches of the North Atlantic/West and those of the global South lies within their vastly different concep-tions of spiritual reality.[15] Having intentionally or unintentionally imbibed the demythologization project of Bultmann, the global North over-emphasizes the role of individuals and structures in the problem of evil, without regard to the extra-human components.[16] Thus, while contemporary thinkers might find it compelling and useful to employ the Apostle's language of powers to personify and spiritualize human institutions, Acolatse brings needed attention

---

14. See: Wink, *Naming the Powers*; *Unmasking the Powers*; *Engaging the Powers*.

15. Acolatse, *Powers, Principalities, and Spirits*, 1.

16. Acolatse, *Powers, Principalities, and Spirits*, 8.

to that which should be obvious: Paul almost certainly believed that the powers were actual spiritual entities.

Acolatse writes, "Scriptural testimony envisions . . . powers as spiritual beings that are inherently evil rather than earthly structures or benign neutral inner spirits of outer poles that become demonic through bad behavior or choice."[17] Thus, while many theologians have gone in strides to recover the language of the powers to describe the corporate reality of evil, the predominant understanding of powers is still often colonized by post-Enlightenment presuppositions that contest the true existence of the powers as spiritual beings.

In his book *Demons*, Michael S. Heiser presents a refreshing understanding of powers and principalities that seems more in line with the "biblical realism" of Acolatse rather than the spiritual nominalism of liberal Protestantism. Notably, Heiser sees the powers as having a peculiarly strong association with the nations of the world. The powers are specifically "territorial spirits" that rule over the gentile nations, enslaving them to idolatry and unbelief.[18] However, because of the work of Christ, the rule of the powers over the gentile nations has been delegitimized and conquered. "Consequently," Heiser writes, "part of the good news of the gospel to those under the gods' dominion was that they were free to turn from those gods and embrace Jesus."[19]

For many readers in a post-Enlightenment culture, such theologizing about evil spirits and demons may seem equal parts regressive and absurd. To rephrase Bultmann's concern, we might suppose that it is impossible to live in a world of space travel, particle colliders, and quantum computing while still believing in the spirit-enchanted cosmos of the New Testament. However, even in a secular age that is presuppositionally biased against the notion of transcendent beings, it is not uncommon to slip into personalizing and spiritualizing the reality of corporate evil in the way we naturally think and speak. The Nazi's were ideologically "possessed."

17. Acolatse, *Powers, Principalities, and Spirits*, 78.

18. Heiser, *Demons*, 22.

19. Heiser, *Demons*, 230.

Commercial greed is "diabolical." Political opponents "demonize" one another in order to win over the "soul" of a nation. Thus, while the category of powers is not necessarily familiar to contemporary readers in the West, our everyday language betrays that we intuitively suspect more about spiritual reality than we are willing to admit. There are aspects of our reality that simply cannot be adequately expressed outside of a spiritual vocabulary.

3

NATIONS AND NATIONALISM

WHAT IS A NATION?

"Nation" is a common term, yet it is notoriously difficult to define.[1] A nation is not directly equivalent to an ethnic people group, a geographic territory, or a state, yet the concept is clearly related to all three realities. Perhaps no purely scientific definition of the nation can be universally agreed upon.[2] Nevertheless, nations have certainly existed, and they continue to exist. So, try to define the nation we must, and try to define the nation we will.

Benedict Anderson memorably understood the nation as "an imagined community."[3] In employing the word "imagined," Anderson does not suggest a lack of reality behind the concept of "nation." Rather, "[the nation] is *imagined* because the fellow members of even the smallest nation will never know most of their fellow-members, meet them, or even hear of them, yet in the minds of each lives the image of their communion."[4] Thus, while other

1. Anthony D. Smith attests that the concept of the "nation" is " . . . the most problematic and contentious term in the field [of nationalism scholarship]." Smith, *Nationalism*, 10.

2. Seton-Watson, *Nations and States*, 5.

3. Anderson, *Imagined Communities*, 6.

4. Anderson, *Imagined Communities*, 8.

scholars stress concepts of shared territoriality[5] or socio-ethnic bonds,[6] Anderson's concept of the "nation" emphasizes the aspect of communal self-consciousness within national identity.

Some scholars, like Anderson, see the possibility of corporate national identity enter the world stage concurrently with the rise of the nation-state and the revolutionary era of the late 1770s.[7] According to this view, national self-consciousness is made possible by the necessary preconditions of wide-spread literacy, the printing press, and the ability to distribute ideas on a mass scale. However, others have noted how national self-consciousness (and therefore the possibility of nationalism) appears to be a perennial and ancient phenomenon.[8] How could national identity be cultivated among members of an imagined community in a premodern era? It is cultivated by shared *religious* practices that foster a common language, a common culture, and a common understanding of history and purpose among a people.[9] For this reason, almost all ancient societies across the globe were centered around an unashamedly symbiotic relationship between civic religion and the state.

From a biblical standpoint, "nations" (Heb. *goy*; Gk. *ethnos*) or "peoples" (Heb. *am*; Gk. *laos*) possess at least four traits that bear a strong resemblance to the qualities highlighted by nationalism scholars of the contemporary era. Scripture tends to present a "nation" as: (1) an ethnically related group of people (2) that dwells

---

5. "The existence of a nation, whether ancient Israel or the modern state, is predicated upon . . . a belief that there exists a territory which belongs only to one people, and that there is a people which belongs to one territory." Grosby, *Nationalism*, 7.

6. "[A nation is] a named human community residing in a perceived homeland, having common myths and a shared history, a distinct public culture, and common laws for all members." Smith, *Nationalism*, 13.

7. Hastings, *The Construction of Nationhood*, 2.

8. Smith prefers to term this view as "perennialism," since such proponents believe that "nationalist ideology . . . [has] always existed in every period of history, and that many nations existed from time immemorial." Smith, *Nationalism*, 53.

9. Hastings, *The Construction of Nationhood*, 175.

in its own territory (3) with its own government and (4) worships its own god or gods.[10] While Israel was constituted as a "nation" (*goy*) in Exodus 19:6, the term often functions as a short-hand expression for people groups who do not know the LORD and instead serve false gods and idols, from whom Israel is to remain separate and distinct (cf. Lev 18:24; 2 Kgs 17:7–20; Jer 10:2–5). Nevertheless, while the "nations" will bear the wrath of God (cf. Jer 10:10), they are also destined to be recipients of his redemption (cf. Ps 67; Isa 25:6–7).[11]

THE CASE FOR (AND AGAINST) NATIONALISM

To some, nationalism means nothing more than the belief that nations possess a natural right to exert self-governance, self-sovereignty, self-determination, and independence.[12] Nationalism is, as Israeli philosopher Yoram Hazony writes, "a principled standpoint that regards the world as governed best when nations are able to chart their own independent course, cultivating their own traditions, and pursuing their own interests without interference."[13] Thus, nationalism may be conceived as that which stands against the oppression of foreign imperialism. Or, to many contemporary nationalists, nationalism simply means putting the interests of the nation first over and against the cumbersome and often self-defeating entanglements of globalism.

But the animating force that propels nationalism is not a general value judgment about how the various nations should relate to

10. Redditt, "Nations." In *EDB* 949. See also: Betram and Schmidt, Ἔθνος, Ἐθνικός." In *TDNT* 364–372.

11. " . . . the nations are both historical bearers of the merciful divine judgment on human sin and also one historical medium of the continuing cultural mandate given by God to the one human race." Storrar, "'Vertigo' or 'Imago'? Nations in the Divine Economy," 5.

12. Note that "sovereignty" and "independence (aseity)" are not just nationalist aspirations and virtues; they are also attributes of God. Even such mild conceptions of nationalism betray a tendency to ascribe god-like qualities to one's nation.

13. Hazony, *The Virtue of Nationalism*, 3.

one another. Rather, the nationalist impulse is rooted in a fervent love—a "natural devotion"—for one's own particular nation.[14] This love arises organically from a shared nativity (the place of one's birth), a shared culture (social values and customs), and a shared heritage (history, language, and often ethnic ancestry) within a given territory or homeland. The inherently communal and shared aspects of national life are what make a nation *our* nation. As Rich Lowry, editor of the *National Review*, writes in *The Case for Nationalism*, "America . . . still has a largely cultural basis. The English language remains a pillar of *our* national identity . . . *Our* rituals and holidays reflect the dominant culture . . . *Our* national heroes, *our* ancestors, are afforded a prized place in *our* collective life. The ascension of George Washington to a quasi-sacred status in *our* country began almost immediately" (emphasis added).[15]

According to its proponents, nationalism should be considered a virtue, not a vice. Nationalism should be eagerly embraced as a unifying force, not a divisive one. After all, by summoning the nation to a unified "sense of mission," nationalism has the power to defend against foreign threats or conquest, it even has the potential (on paper, at least) to oppose racism and other divisive forms of "sub-national" loyalty.[16]

But there is a fly in the ointment. If nationalism is fueled by and founded upon a common love for one's culture and nationality, this raises the questions: "Whose culture? Whose nationality?"

What if nationalism's definition of culture implicitly or explicitly alienates some citizens from membership of their own nation? What if the notion of nationality becomes inextricably woven with ethnicity or even subscription to a preferred political ideology?

14. Lowry, *The Case for Nationalism*, 13.

15. Lowry, *The Case for Nationalism*, 19. Note that Lowry uses the term "quasi-sacred" in a positive sense, as well as the word "ascension" (an inherently Christological term) in reference to George Washington. Chapter 13 will make further observations on this tendency within nationalism to portray national leaders in messianic categories.

16. Lowry, *The Case for Nationalism*, 15.

These are not unmerited concerns. Under Hitler, Jewish Germans suddenly found themselves outside of German nation because of their ethnicity. Political dissidents similarly found themselves outside of German nation because of their ideas. Many lost their lives in Nazism's fervor to purify the German nation.

"But Nazism was not real nationalism," the nationalist might say. Hitler simply exploited nationalistic tropes through his charismatic leadership.[17] Yet, this line of argumentation is about as convincing as claim that Stalinism wasn't real communism. The haunting truth is that Hitler's nationalism was a unifying force that inspired both great and terrible deeds. Indeed, it is both self-deceptive and special pleading to deny that the same nationalism that built the autobahn also built the camp of Buchenwald.

One might see the beginnings of such a nationalism at play when Americans, who have known no other homeland, are told to "go back" where they came from. Or perhaps, we might consider the implications of describing an opposing political perspective of fellow citizens as "un-American."

Simply said, nationalism casts a vision of the nation in exclusionary, adversarial, and often absolutist terms. It determines that the nation must value and protect *this* culture, not *that* one; *this* nationality, not *that* one, with little room for nuance. Because of this polarizing impulse, nationalism naturally cultivates resentment toward and scapegoating of those it envisions as "outside of the nation." This is the dark price nationalism must pay in order to foster unity among those it conceives as being "in the nation."[18]

17. Lowry, *The Case for Nationalism*, 21.

18. It is for this reason that I am unconvinced by Rich Lowry's claim that there was nothing "nationalistic about [President Trump's] initial reluctance to unambiguously denounce the far-right protests in Charlottesville" (Lowry, *The Case for Nationalism*, 5). Trump's brand of nationalism inherently appealed to and was celebrated by the self-identified white nationalist organizers of this rally turned riot. To quote a cliché, nationalism's appeal to ethnic or ideological supremacy is not a bug—it's a feature.

NATIONALISM AS A RELIGION

I am not a political scientist or sociologist. More qualified voices can speak to the implications of nationalism on public policy or society at large.

I am a pastor. So, what concerns me is the inherently religious language and tropes that nationalists—*regardless of their nationality*—unfailingly utilize when they make their appeals. It disturbs me how over the course of human history, nationalism consistently bends the "natural devotion" to one's nation into something indistinguishable from worship. As Pastor Timothy Keller has observed, whenever a good thing becomes an ultimate thing, whenever something absorbs our hearts and imaginations more than God, that thing—whatever it may be—has effectively turned into an idol.[19]

Thus, I contend that nationalism is best defined religiously. Nationalism is the exaltation of a nation (or conception of a nation) to a place of highest allegiance, concern, and devotion.[20] It refers to a constellation of beliefs culminating in the nation being viewed as the highest good and ultimate love. In this way, nationalism is less of a political ideology and more of a "species of religion,"[21] in which devotion to the nation becomes "a paramount, a supreme loyalty, commanding all others."[22]

To view nationalism in spiritual or religious terms is not to wage an unfair or unwarranted criticism against nationalist thought. Rather, to classify nationalism as a form of spiritual devotion is to take nationalist proponents on their own terms. In

19. Keller, *Counterfeit Gods*, xviii.

20. Nationalism is a word that has a spectrum of meaning in both popular society and scholarship. While my definition of nationalism fits firmly within the spectrum of scholarly literature on nationalism and can be justified by primary sources, it is (admittedly) an inherently critical definition. Nevertheless, I would argue that even mitigated definitions of nationalism betray an impulse for autonomy and self-sovereignty that point toward a Babel-like exaltation of the "earthly city" over and against the kingdom of God.

21. Smith, *Nationalism*, 27.

22. Hayes, *Nationalism*, 10.

Qu'est-ce qu'une nation?, French nationalist Ernest Renan declares that "A nation is a soul, a spiritual principle."[23] Intentionally appealing to religious language, Renan sees the nation as the "end product" of collective "sacrifice and devotion" of a people who possess a common legacy regarding the past and a consent to live together in the present.[24] Nations are not eternal or given realities, but they must be preserved for the sake of liberty.[25] In a statement that fits just as well on the ancient plains of Shinar as it does in eighteenth-century Paris, Renan announces: "A great aggregation of men, with a healthy spirit and warmth of heart, creates a moral conscience which is called a nation. When this moral conscience proves its strength by sacrifices that demand abdication of the individual for the benefit of the community, it is legitimate and has the right to exist."[26]

However, one does not need to hold such absolutized beliefs about his or her nation in order to serve as a contributing member or citizen of one's nation. Indeed, one can be a patriot without necessarily being a nationalist. For this reason, many authors have found it useful to make a distinction between patriotism and nationalism.[27] For scholar Steven Grosby,

> ... patriotism implies a commitment to the well-being of one's country, it provides the basis for working out the differences involving reasonable compromise between members of the nation and their differing conceptions of what the nation should be out of a concern for promoting that well-being ... When one divides the world into two irreconcilable and warring camps—one's own nation in opposition to all other nations—where the latter are viewed as implacable enemies, then in contrast to patriotism, there is the ideology of *nationalism*. Nationalism repudiates civility and the differences that it tolerates by

23. Renan, *Qu'est-ce qu'une nation?*, 26.

24. Renan, *Qu'est-ce qu'une nation?*, 26.

25. Renan, *Qu'est-ce qu'une nation?*, 26.

26. Renan, *Qu'est-ce qu'une nation?*, 26.

27. An early use of this distinction between "nationalism" and "patriotism" appears in Orwell, *Notes on Nationalism*, 2

attempting to eliminate all differing views and interests
for the sake of one vision of what that nation has been
and should be.[28]

As such, when a version of nationalism becomes dominant in
a given state, it possesses the potential to threaten the individual
liberty of those with dissenting voices.[29] Defined this way, patriotism may be seen as a necessary precondition for a democratic society to promote justice for all against the tyranny of the majority.
However, nationalism perverts justice when justice runs contrary
to the prevailing (or preferred) national culture.[30]

Theologically speaking, patriotism may be understood as
a rightly ordered love for one's nation, whereas nationalism is
a disordered love for one's nation that has twisted into idolatry.
Some nationalist proponents decry distinguishing patriotism from
nationalism as unwarranted, and argue that the terms should be
interchangeable.[31] Yet, the distinction between patriotism and nationalism within common language (along with their respective
positive and negative connotations) reveals that at some level we
intuit a vital difference between rightly and wrongly ordered love
for one's nation.

C.S. Lewis explores the difference between rightly and
wrongly ordered love for one's nation in *The Screwtape Letters*. In
this fictionalized collection of letters between Screwtape, a high-
ranking demon, and Wormwood, Screwtape's novice nephew, who
is attempting to lead his first "patient" (a human) away from the
dreaded influence of the "Enemy" (God).

In one such letter, Screwtape responds to Wormwood's question regarding whether or not the demon should influence his
patient toward extreme patriotism or extreme pacifism. Set during
the World War 2 era, Wormwood wonders whether the patient
should be devoted to a vision of Great Britain defined by mili-
taristic interventionism against the Nazis (what Lewis here calls

28. Grosby, *Nationalism*, 17.

29. Grosby, *Nationalism*, 5.

30. Koyzis, *Political Visions and Illusions*, 114.

31. Lowry, *The Case for Nationalism*, 16.

"patriotism"), or whether the patient should be devoted to a vision of Great Britain defined by principled isolationism (what Lewis here terms as "pacifism").

Surprisingly, Screwtape does not hold rigid convictions on the matter. He does, however, care deeply about the degree of the patient's devotion to one cause or the other: "All extremes, except extreme devotion to the enemy, are to be encouraged."[32] In other words, Screwtape's demonic agenda does not prefer one political vision of the British nation over another—whether interventionist or isolationist. The senior demon simply desires for the patient to adopt a religious level of fervor and fanaticism for whichever version of political perspective he chooses.

Screwtape will even go so far as to instruct Wormwood on how to instrumentalize the patient's Christian faith toward cultivating extremism:

> Let him begin by treating the Patriotism or the Pacifism as a part of his religion. Then let him, under the influence of the partisan spirit, come to regard it as the most important part. Then quietly and gradually nurse him to the stage at which religion becomes merely part of the "cause," in which Christianity is valued chiefly because of the excellent arguments it can produce in favor of the British war-effort or of Pacifism .... Once you have made the World an end, and faith a means, you have almost won your man, and it makes if very little difference what kind of worldly end he is pursuing. Provided that meetings, pamphlets, policies, movements, and crusades, matter more to him than prayers and sacraments and charity, he is ours—the more "religious" (on those terms) the more securely ours.

To be clear, Lewis is not against having an opinion on such issues. He does not view matters of politics or war as unimportant. Indeed, he even wrote an essay entitled, "Why I am Not a Pacifist."[33] However, Lewis is showing that when we exalt our na-

---

32. Lewis, *The Screwtape Letters*, 32.
33. Lewis, *The Weight of Glory*, 64–90.

tion (or conception of a nation) to the highest place of devotion, we have succumbed to nothing less than a demonic temptation that is at odds with devotion to God.

NATIONALISM AS A VARIEGATED PHENOMENON

The previous example of *The Screwtape Letters* sheds light on another key aspect of nationalism, which is its *variegated* nature. Nationalist ideology is not limited to any one nation, ethnicity, or political ideology. Indeed, history has shown as many forms of nationalism as there were forms of Baal worship in the ancient Levant. Political scientist David T. Koyzis observes, " . . . nationalism differs from one time and place the next. Nationalisms are utterly different from each other because the focus of each is utterly different."[34] Thus, nationalism scholars often distinguish "ethnic nationalism" (a nationalism rooted in racial or ethnic identity) from "civic nationalism" (a nationalism rooted in political ideology).[35]

Just as different ethnicities can furnish differing ethnic nationalisms, so too, different political ideologies can furnish differing civic nationalisms. Adolph Hitler, Joseph Stalin, and Joseph McCarthy held widely dissimilar political ideologies, but all three were nationalists. As renowned nationalism scholar Anthony D. Smith notes, "Nationalist ideology is . . . structurally incapable of dealing with . . . major political issues as social justice, the distribution of resources, or conflict management. In fact, nationalism is often not a distinct ideology at all, as it simply fills out the more mainstream ideologies, such as liberalism, socialism, and conservatism."[36] Herein lies another reason for viewing nationalism not as a political ideology, but a religious shell that contains and promotes the interests of an ethnic group or a particular political ideology in regards to the nation.

34. Koyzis, *Political Visions and Illusions*, 97.

35. Smith, *Nationalism*, 42–46.

36. Smith, *Nationalism*, 26–27.

What then of varieties of nationalism that are explicitly enmeshed with a traditional religion? How should we locate something like Christian nationalism?

As the forthcoming chapters will make clear, Christian nationalism is a form of religious syncretism. Syncretism is an attempt to combine inherently different or opposite religious or philosophical systems, doctrines, and practices.[37] Gnosticism was a form of syncretism between Christianity and Neoplatonic philosophy. In the Old Testament, King Jeroboam led the Northern Kingdom of Israel (or Samaria) into apostasy by promoting a syncretistic religion that fused the worship of Yahweh with the worship of Baal.

But just because you slap the name of Yahweh on a golden calf doesn't make worshipping an idol acceptable. Likewise, just because a politician commandeers a Bible verse to promote an ideology doesn't make a nation or political platform Christian. In fact, for shrewd politicians, Christian nationalism is nothing more than an expedient tool or trick that co-opts Christian language and sentiments for a nationalist cause. It is nationalism with the veneer of Jesus, which serves nationalism by granting divine sanction, authority, and the aura of orthodoxy to the cause of the nation.

But admittedly, this trick works well. There are disturbing spiritual reasons *why* this trick works well, and has done so for a very, very long time.

37. *ODCC* 1579.

Part II

ANCIENT ORIGINS

4

It Began at Babel

A QUEST FOR ORIGINS

The Apostle Paul did not live in an intellectual vacuum or a pristine cultural milieu. He was a Roman citizen, familiar with Greek poets and philosophers, educated by the noble Gamaliel, and, above all, a Jew "circumcised on the eighth day, of the people of Israel, of the tribe of Benjamin, a Hebrew of Hebrews; as to the law, a Pharisee" (Phil 3:5). As such, Paul's vocabulary and ideas, have a rich history and heritage that are worthy of exploration.

As already mentioned in the chapter 2, when Paul speaks of "principalities and powers," his word choice conveys a consistent suggestion not only of personal evil forces, but also forces that seem to possess dominion over peoples and territories. But who are these powers, and where did they come from? The chapters of this section will put forward a theory of the origins behind Paul's conception of powers that will underscore the intimate connection between such powers and pagan nations.

BABEL AND THE ORIGIN OF NATIONS

The Bible locates the origin of nations in Genesis 10 and 11, which respectively recount the "Table of Nations" and the "Tower of

Babel." Chapter 10 functions as a genealogy of the post-diluvian progeny of Noah's sons: Shem, Ham, and Japheth. When tallied together, this account adds up to seventy names that refer to the nations of ancient Israel's known world. The number seventy (a multiple of seven and ten) indicates a sense of completeness, representing "the whole of the world's families . . . under the eye of God."[1] Thus, each nation suggests an ethnic group of a shared ancestry, a shared "land" (Gen 10:5, 20, 31–32), and a shared "language" (10:5, 20, 31).

Nestled in this list is a brief depiction of Nimrod, known as a "mighty hunter," and the "first on the earth to be a mighty man" (10:8–9). The only individual person deemed worthy of description in this list, Nimrod is a king (melek), for to him belongs a "kingdom" (mamlakht).[2] Moreover, as a type of anti-Abraham, he appears to be the patriarch of Babel in the land of Shinar and Nineveh in the land of Assyria (10:10–11), nations who will one day wreak destruction upon the ancient Near East, including the people of Israel and Judah. This mention of Babel, as well as Nimrod's name (which means "we shall rebel"), foreshadows the coming episode in Genesis 11:1–9.[3]

Babel is the literal "genesis" (reshith, 10:10; cf. 1:1)[4] of Nimrod's kingdom, and it becomes the setting for gentile rebellion against the LORD. Here, the proto-Babylonians announce, " . . . Come, let us build ourselves a city and a tower with its top in the heavens, and let us make a name for ourselves, lest we be dispersed over the face of the whole earth" (11:4). While seemingly innocuous to some modern ears, this statement reveals both pride and disobedience. By wanting to make "a name" for themselves, the builders of Babel are attempting to establish a corporate identity that is unconnected to their creator. Through their own collective creation, they want

---

1. Mathews, *Genesis 1–11:26*, 430.

2. Interestingly, Genesis 10:10 is the first instance in the Bible in which the word "kingdom" (*mamlakhah*) appears.

3. Waltke and Fredricks, *Genesis*, 169.

4. *HALOT* 1169.

to establish significance and a type of immortality.[5] While men like Noah, Abraham, Isaac, and Jacob "build" (*bnh*) altars to Yahweh (Gen 8:20; 12:7, 8; 13:18; 22:9; 35:7), Nimrod and his nationalist cohorts "build" (*bnh*) a city and a vaunted tower as an altar to the worship of their corporate glory (11:4).[6] Even more, in blatant disobedience to the command to Genesis 1:28 to "fill the earth and subdue it" the builders of Babel refuse to be dispersed across the face of the earth (11:4).[7] Rather than spreading out to bring forth the kingdom of God on earth, the people of Babel desire to bring the kingdom of man to heaven. Alternatively, the tower of Babel may also be viewed as a mechanism to bring God down to man, so that he might be more effectively managed to enact the will of his worshippers.

However, God lives in heaven; he does as he pleases (cf. Ps 115:3). He will not be co-opted, coerced, or managed. As high as the tower of Babel may rise, God has to come down to see it (Gen 11:5). Seeing the destructive force this kingdom of man possesses, the LORD confuses the languages of the proud builders and disperses them over the face of all the earth (11:6–9). Though abandoned for a time, the city of Babel will rise again to exert its will upon the earth. Even more, the gentile nations will scatter across the earth, each seeking a homeland, each seeking to make a name for themselves, and each building their own towers, their own altars to the city of man.

Nevertheless, although dispersed after the rebellion at Babel, God does not devote the gentile nations to destruction. In Genesis 11:31—12:3, he calls childless Abram out of Ur of the Chaldeans—out of the nations, so to speak. Through Abram, God will create *ex nihilo* a new family that would be destined to grow into a new nation. God will bless Abram (later called Abraham) and his offspring, and through Abraham's blessed family, "all the families of the earth shall be blessed" (Gen 12:3).[8] God scatters the nations

5. Waltke and Fredricks, *Genesis*, 179.

6. Waltke and Fredricks, Genesis, 170.

7. Greidanus, *Preaching Christ from Genesis*, 122.

8. The blessing of the nations through the family of Abraham is a recurring

in judgment. But from the nations, he calls a new nation unto himself, so that, through this one nation, redemption and restoration might come to all nations.

However, Babel and Abraham's family will continue to represent two contrasting societies throughout Scripture. The difference between these two societies is fundamentally rooted in two different loves. As Augustine of Hippo famously wrote centuries later, "Accordingly, two cities have been formed by two loves: the earthly by the love of self, even to the contempt of God; the heavenly by the love of God, even to the contempt of self. The former, in a word, glories in itself, the latter in the Lord."[9]

DEUTERONOMY 32 AND THE ORIGIN OF POWERS

Deuteronomy 32:8–9 provides a theological commentary on the Babel event and the subsequent call of Abram: "When the Most High gave to the nations their inheritance, when he divided mankind, he fixed the borders of the peoples according to the number of the sons of God. But the LORD's portion is his people, Jacob his allotted heritage" (Deut 32:8–9).[10] As a whole, the "Song of Moses" of Deuteronomy 32 represents a plea to the people of Israel to behold the faithfulness of God, the futility of false gods, and the sacred privilege of what it means to be Yahweh's chosen people. However, verses 8 and 9 reveal previously unknown knowledge concerning the cosmic and spiritual reality behind the origin of nations that bears profound implications upon the present study.

---

refrain of emphasis in Genesis. See also: Gen 18:18, 26:4, 28:14.

9. Augustine of Hippo, "The City of God," bk. 14, ch. 28.

10. Some English translations, such as the *NIV, NASB,* and *NKJV,* render the last phrase of Deuteronomy 32:8 as "according to the sons of Israel," which is based on the Masoretic Text. However, the combined witness of the LXX (*angelōn theou*) and the DSS 4QDeutJ (*vene elohim*) indicate that "according to the sons of God" is the preferred reading. Heiser has convincingly presented the exegetical and logical problems with the former translation, suggesting that the "sons of Israel" represents a scribal alteration, motivated from a theological concern that the earlier (original) reading suggests divine plurality. See: Heiser, "Deuteronomy 32:8 and the Sons of God," 52–74.

Functioning together, verses 8 and 9 create a stark contrast: Yahweh has taken Israel to be his portion (9), but the gentile nations have been allotted to the "sons of God," lesser gods, who seem to be presented as angels of Yahweh's heavenly host.[11]

Does Deuteronomy 32:8–9, thus, betray evidence of polytheism (or even henotheism) in ancient Israelite religion? By no means! The "sons of God" are *created* spiritual beings. They possess a measure of power and authority, but only in a derivative sense. They do not bear the divine attributes of omnipotence, omniscience, omnipresence, and aseity. Nevertheless, Deuteronomy presents the "sons of God" as real, personal, spiritual beings who are connected to the nations, and who are ultimately worshipped by the nations as patron deities.[12] Yet, although none of these foreign gods guided Israel through the wilderness (32:12), Israel will provoke Yahweh to anger by falling prey to the worship of the gods of the nations: "They stirred him to jealousy with strange gods; with abominations they provoked him to anger. They sacrificed to demons that were no gods, to gods they had never known, to new gods that had come recently, whom your fathers had never dreaded" (32:16–17). Here again, the text insists that these "demons" (*shedim*) are not figments of pagan imagination. Rather, they are real spiritual entities. However, their claim to divinity is clearly a deceptive pretense. The ruse of these false gods will not last forever. The Most High will take vengeance upon his "adversaries" and all false gods will bow before him (32:41, 43).[13]

---

11. Heiser, *Demons*, 148.

12. Block, *The Gods of the Nations*, 29.

13. Did the "sons of god" lead the nations into idolatry, did the nations entice the "sons of god" into rebellion against Yahweh, or do the nations and their false gods collaborate in a mutual rebellion against God? Deuteronomy 32 does not explicitly give an answer. Perhaps God's allotment of the nations to their gods should be viewed in the same line of thought expressed in Romans 1:18–25, wherein God gives the nations over to the false gods/idols they so desire. Whatever the case, Deuteronomy 32 seems to teach that the "sons of God" are not only associated with the nations but that they also *rule* over the nations. Moreover, through the rule of these spiritual forces, the gentiles fall further and further into deception and wickedness.

Evidence for this understanding of Deuteronomy 32 appears in writings of the Second Temple period.[14] For example, Ben Sirach states, "He appointed a ruler for every nation, but Israel is the Lord's own portion" (Sir 17:17, NRSV). An even more explicit reference appears in the book of Jubilees:

> He knew them, but He chose Israel to be His people. And He sanctified it, and gathered it from amongst all the children of men; for there are many nations and many peoples, and all are His, and over all hath He placed spirits in authority to lead them astray from Him. But over Israel He did not appoint any angel or spirit, for He alone is their ruler, and He will preserve them and require them at the hand of His angels and His spirits, and at the hand of all His powers in order that He may preserve them and bless them, and that they may be His and He may be theirs from henceforth forever.[15]

As a simple short-hand phrase, this line of thought can may termed as the "Deuteronomy 32 worldview." It is, in the words of Old Testament scholar Michael S. Heiser, the " . . . biblical explanation as to how humanity's direct relationship to the creator God morphed into the worship of other gods."[16]

---

14. The Second Temple period refers to the period of time in Jewish history between 516 B.C. (when the returned exiles rebuilt the Temple of Jerusalem) and A.D. 70 (when the Roman legions destroyed the Temple of Jerusalem).

15. Charles, "The Book of Jubilees," 37.

16. Heiser, *Demons*, 150.

5

PUT AWAY THE GODS
YOUR FATHERS SERVED

THE "DEUTERONOMY 32 WORLDVIEW" IN
ANCIENT JEWISH THOUGHT

Several Old Testament passages seem to indicate the people of ancient Israel presupposed the tenets of the "Deuteronomy 32 worldview" in the way they understood the nature of reality. As Joshua concludes the Canaanite conquest and nears the end of his life, he famously commands the children of Israel:

> Now therefore fear the LORD and serve him in sincerity and in faithfulness. Put away the gods that your fathers served beyond the River and in Egypt, and serve the LORD. And if it is evil in your eyes to serve the LORD, choose this day whom you will serve, whether the gods your fathers served in the region beyond the River, or the gods of the Amorites in whose land you dwell. But as for me and my house, we will serve the LORD (Josh 24:14–15).

Primarily, Joshua exhorts the people of God toward a singular allegiance to the LORD. However, compliance with this exhortation necessarily includes a rejection of all other "gods" (*elohim*). Earlier in this speech, Joshua states that even the great patriarch

Abraham's family had once served false gods while they were still in Mesopotamia (24:2), and that the Israelites had also fallen prey to the worship of the gods of Egypt (24:14). By recounting this history of spiritual infidelity, Joshua warns the people of his own generation that they are not above falling under the dominion of gods associated with the territory where they now reside. They must intentionally "put away" these false gods and choose faithfulness and fear of the LORD.

The Old Testament includes numerous other examples of gentile gods ruling over gentile peoples and lands, most of which serve the same hortatory function as Joshua 24:14–15.[1] However, Psalm 82 and Daniel 10 present two Old Testament passages that are uniquely associated with and further illuminate the "Deuteronomy 32 worldview."[2]

PSALM 82

Psalm 82 presents a scene of a cosmic courtroom: "God has taken his place in the divine council; in the midst of the gods he holds judgment" (Ps 82:1). "God" (*elohim*) takes his place in the midst of other "gods" (*elohim*). While both Yahweh and the gods of his divine council are similar in that they are spiritual beings, Yahweh possesses undeniable supremacy over all other gods.[3] God is alone is the creator; the so-called "gods" are part of his creation.[4]

---

1. See also: Deut 6:14; Judg 6:10; 11:24, 16:23; 2 Kgs 17:26–27; 2 Chr 25:14, 20, 32:14–17; Jer 2:11, 49:1; Mic 4:5.

2. G.B. Caird, Daniel I. Block, Clinton E. Arnold, and Michael S. Heiser represent scholars who observe a significant link between Deuteronomy 32:8 and the passages of Psalm 82 and Daniel 10. For a dissenting view concerning the conceptual relationship between these texts see: Walton and Walton, *Demons and Spirits in Biblical Theology*, 186–208.

3. See also: "Let the heavens praise your wonders, O LORD, your faithfulness in the assembly of the holy ones! For who in the skies can be compared to the LORD? Who among the heavenly beings is like the LORD, a God greatly to be feared in the council of the holy ones, and awesome above all who are around him?" (Ps 89:5–7).

4. In a similar vein, Psalm 148:1–5 explicitly describes "angels" and "hosts,"

As the just and sovereign LORD, Yahweh accuses the gods of promoting injustice (82:2), of failing to uphold the vulnerable (82:3–4), of causing their subjects to be effectively blinded to the reality of God (82:5a; cf. 2 Cor 4:4), and of perpetuating brokenness in God's good creation (82:5b). For these crimes, God charges the accused of cosmic treason, even sentencing them to death and destruction.[5] Echoing the word-choice of Deuteronomy 32:8, Yahweh pronounces " . . . You are gods, sons of the Most High, all of you; nevertheless, like men you shall die, and fall like any prince" (82:6–7). The unjust powers will fall, and God will "arise" (*qumah*)[6] as the rightful judge of the earth (82:8). The reign of the wicked gods will come to an end, and the LORD, the God of Israel, will "inherit"[7] all nations.[8]

Significantly, Psalm 82 presumes that the reader is aware that there are lesser gods who possess dominion over the gentile nations. These gods oppress the people of the nations and obscure them from knowing the true Creator God (Yahweh). However, Psalm 82 is also prophetic. A day is coming when God will "arise" to dethrone these spiritual beings and reclaim the nations as his own inheritance. As future chapters will explore, this exact framework forms the logic for how Paul interprets Christ's victory over the powers.

---

members of the divine council, as "created" beings. Interestingly, the LXX translates "hosts" (*tseva*) in 148:1 as "powers" (*dynameis*), which forms a clear lexical link between the Old Testament's presentation of the divine council and Paul's understanding of "powers" (*dynameōs*) (cf. Eph 1:21).

5. God's judgment upon the heavenly host also appears in Isaiah 24:21 and 34:2.

6. Note the conceptual link between "arise" (*qum*) and the later doctrines of the resurrection and ascension of Christ, which for Paul, are connected to delegitimizing the authority of the powers over the nations.

7. This appears to be another direct lexical reference to "inheritance" (*nhl*) in Deuteronomy 32:8.

8. Hossfeld and Zenger, *Psalms 2*, 332.

DANIEL 10

Perhaps the most obvious Old Testament narrative example of the "Deuteronomy 32 worldview" occurs in Daniel 10. After three weeks of fervent prayer and fasting, a now-elderly Daniel beholds an extraordinary vision along the banks of the Tigris River (Dan 10:1–6; cf. Ezek 1:26–28; Rev 1:12–16). [9] The sight and sound of this "man" overwhelms the prophet so that he can no longer stand (Dan 10:7–10). A hand reaches out to touch him, and a voice speaks:

> And he said to me, "O Daniel, man greatly loved, understand the words that I speak to you, and stand upright, for now I have been sent to you." And when he had spoken this word to me, I stood up trembling. Then he said to me, "Fear not, Daniel, for from the first day that you set your heart to understand and humbled yourself before your God, your words have been heard, and I have come because of your words. The prince of the kingdom of Persia withstood me twenty-one days, but Michael, one of the chief princes, came to help me, for I was left there with the kings of Persia, and came to make you understand what is to happen to your people in the latter days. For the vision is for days yet to come" (Dan 10:11–14).

Two important questions emerge in relation to the text: who is the speaker, and who is the "prince of the kingdom of Persia" who "withstands"[10] the speaker for twenty-one days?

Scholars do not agree concerning the identity of the speaker of in verses 11 through 14. Some identify the speaker as "the Angel of the LORD (i.e., the LORD Himself) who here makes war on behalf of his own against the spirit of the heathen world powers."[11] Other commentators, however, have accepted the hypothesis that the speaker is merely an angelic interpreter, perhaps even Gabriel,

9. Miller, *Daniel*, 281–282.

10. The LXX translates "withstand" (Heb. *omed*) in 10:13 as "*antheistēkei*," which is the same verb Paul uses in Eph 6:13 in relation to spiritual warfare.

11. Young, *Daniel*, 227.

who has already played an interpretative role earlier in Daniel (8:15–6; 9:21).[12]

As to the identity of the "prince of the kingdom of Persia," some have thought that this "prince" refers to the human king of Persia.[13] However, the great majority of scholars view the prince of Persia and the "prince of Greece" (10:20) as referring to spiritual beings who bear a measure of spiritual dominion over their respective realms. Old Testament scholar John J. Collins notes: "By analogy with Michael it is clear that the 'princes' of Greece and Persia are the patron angels of these nations."[14] Notably, Theodotion's Greek translation of Daniel translates "prince" (Heb. *sar*) in this passage as "ruler" (Gk. *archē*), a term that "all four of the Gospel writers and Paul [use] either for Satan or for evil spirit powers."[15] For this reason, it may be reasonable to conclude that, the "princes" of Daniel 10:13, 20 are of the same class as Paul's "rulers of this age" in 1 Corinthians 2:6, 8. It seems equally reasonable to equate the "princes" of Daniel 10:13, 21 with the "sons of God" in Deuteronomy 32:8.

The "Deuteronomy 32 worldview" may illuminate even more mystery in Daniel 10, namely the identity of the speaker in verses 10:11–14. The most natural reading of the text would indicate that the speaker of 10:11–14 is the same being that the prophet Daniel sees is the vision of 10:5–6. However, this identification is not without problems. Those who identify the speaker of these verses with an unprefaced angelic interpreter tend to ground this supposition on theological concerns more than on exegetical grounds. After all, one might wonder, how could it be possible for the Prince of Persia to withstand the power of the almighty LORD?

12. Miller, *Daniel*, 283.

13. Calvin, *Daniel*, 252.

14. Collins, "Prince." In *DDD* 663.

15. The Theodotion LXX was the most prominent version of the LXX in first century Ephesus and Asia Minor, which may account for Paul's preference for "*archē*" in letters such as Ephesians and Colossians. Arnold, *Powers of Darkness*, 63.

However, according to Deuteronomy 32:8, the "Most High" himself allotted the nations to the "sons of God." The princes of Persia and Greece hold their dominion, not despite of but *because of* Yahweh's absolute sovereignty over the nations. One need not presume that the prince of Persia's ability to withstand Yahweh represents a genuine challenge to Yahweh's omnipotence. Rather, it may be that the prince of Persia merely contests Yahweh's intrusion into his territory on the basis of Yahweh's own allotment. In other words, the prince of Persia contests Yahweh's presence in Persia because, for the time being, he possesses a legitimate claim to dominion over this nation. Nevertheless, the Apostle Paul will later show how such claims that the powers once held over the nations has come to a definitive end through the person and work of Jesus Christ.

6

THE GODS OF THE NATIONS

THE GODS OF THE NATIONS

While the prevalence of the "Deuteronomy 32 worldview" is well attested in ancient Jewish thought, such a perspective was far from being an idiosyncratic view of the Jewish people. Both ancient Near East sources and the Old Testament indicate that other people groups of the ancient Near East interpreted their reality through the lens of this "cosmic geography."[1] In his book *The Gods of the Nations*, Daniel I. Block argues that national identity in the ancient Near East was inextricably bound to a nation's patron deity: " . . . it is impossible to examine the relationship of a god and his/her subjects in isolation from the ties of both deity and population to the land. Furthermore, a people's ties to its homeland cannot be understood without reference to some measure of divine involvement."[2] In other words, to be a Moabite was to worship Chemosh; to be an Ammonite was to worship Milcom/Molech; to be an Edomite was to worship Qos.[3] While those living in the

1. "Cosmic geography" is another phrase that Heiser and other scholars use to describe the "Deuteronomy 32 worldview." See: Heiser, *The Unseen Realm*, 116–122.

2. Block, *The Gods of the Nations*, 20.

3. Block illustrates this point by a careful analysis of theophoric names,

post-Enlightenment West might distinguish worshipping the *god of a nation* from worshipping the *nation as a god*, to a resident of the ancient Near East, this would be a distinction without a difference.

For example, in the *Mesha Steele* (c. 830 B.C.), which is the earliest known extra-biblical reference to Israel, King Mesha of Moab celebrates a military triumph over the King Ahab of Israel by characterizing his victory as a victory of Chemosh. Ahab's father, King Omri, had "humbled Moab for many days, for Chemosh was angry at his land." [4] However, Mesha casts himself as a loyal servant of Chemosh who devotes the blood and bounty of wars won to his patron god: "I slew all the inhabitants of the town, a satiation (intoxication) for Chemosh and Moab."[5] Indeed, the Moabite king's devotion to Chemosh is so fanatical that 2 Kings 3:26–27 testifies that he sacrificed his own son and heir to Chemosh to secure victory for his nation.

This intimate linkage between ethnic identity and worship of one's national patron god shows the extraordinary nature of gentile conversions in the Old Testament. When Ruth announces to Naomi, "Your people shall be my people," she is already implying "your God [shall be] my God" (Ruth 1:16). By attaching herself to Naomi's people and homeland, Ruth confesses her allegiance to Yahweh and renounces loyalty to Chemosh.[6] Moreover, when the Syrian general Naaman transfers his devotion to Yahweh (2 Kings 5:15–17), he requests that he can take Israelite soil back to Syria "so that he can worship Yahweh on Yahweh's own territory, even though Naaman lives in the domain of the god Rimmon."[7] Both Ruth and Naaman recognize that, in order to join themselves

---

which were "in effect expressions of faith, reflecting the spiritual allegiance of the bearer." This tendency was also reflected in Hebrew theophoric names as well, with many names including Yah, Yahweh, and El. See: Block, *The Gods of the Nations*, 40–45.

4. "The Moabite Stone." In *ANET* 320–321.

5. "The Moabite Stone." In *ANET* 320–321.

6. Block, *The Gods of the Nations*, 39.

7. Heiser, *The Unseen Realm*, 118.

to Yahweh, they must no longer live as the gentiles do (cf. Eph 4:17). In devoting themselves to the God of Israel, they no must no longer exalt their nation to a place of highest allegiance, concern, and devotion. In modern terminology, they must forsake their former nationalism. They now belong to a new God, a new people, and a new land.

Conversely, one of the more insidious instances in the Old Testament of ancient religious nationalism at play occurs in Isaiah 36—37, when the Assyrian armies of Sennacherib invade the kingdom of Judah. At the beginning of chapter 36, the "Rabshakeh" arrives before the gates of Jerusalem, with a mighty army behind him. He is the spokesman of Sennacherib, the Assyrian king. Characterized as a dark-mirror version of Isaiah the prophet, the Rabshakeh has been sent and commissioned to declare the word of the Assyrian king.[8] He speaks in a familiar prophetic formula, "Thus, says the great king, the king of Assyria" (Isa 36:4). The reader is thus alerted to the spiritual undertones of this moment. More than a mere political leader or military commander, the Rabshakeh represents a rival god of a rival religion.

The nation of Assyria was named after the god Ashur, who was considered to be the spiritual personification of the Assyrian empire.[9]

---

8. The role of an Old Testament prophet was first and foremost to represent God, likened to an ambassador sent by a suzerain overlord to his vassal. In the early days of the monarchy, the prophet served in a royal advisory role, helping the vassal (Israel) remain faithful to his treaty (the Mosaic law) with the suzerain (Yahweh). However, later in the history of Israel, the prophet serves more so in the role of Yahweh's "covenant prosecutor" who specifies how Israel, as a wayward vassal, has broken the terms of the covenant and must repent or else face the consequences of the covenant curses. As a representative of the Most High King of heaven, the prophet was called directly by God, empowered by God, and had access to the divine council of God's royal court in heaven. For a more extensive treatment of the role of the prophet, see Williams, *The Prophet and His Message*, 49–71.

9. Radner, *Ancient Assyria*, 3

The God Ashur (Assur). 865–850 B.C.E. Originally from the North-West
Palace of Ashurnasirpal II at Nimrud (Biblical Calah; ancient Kalhu),
modern-day Ninawa Governorate, Iraq, now housed in The British Museum,
London. Photograph courtesy of Osama Shukir Muhammed Amin.

For the Assyrians, Ashur was to be worshipped and served above
all other loyalties. In a pagan distortion of both the Davidic covenant in 2 Samuel 7 and the divine mandate for humanity in
Genesis 1:28, Assyrian religion cast the Assyrian king as Ashur's
anointed representative on earth, who accomplished the will of
Ashur by expanding the dominion of the Assyrian empire. The
temple of Ashur even housed idols taken from temples of nations
that Assyria had conquered, as a representation of all the gods of
the various nations bowing down to Ashur.[10] The Rabshakeh is,
thus, a false prophet of a false messiah of a false religion of nationalistic imperialism.

This background informs the taunt of the Rabshakeh, who
blatantly states that the Assyrians intend to assert supremacy, not
only over Judah, but over Yahweh himself: "Beware lest Hezekiah
mislead you by saying, 'The LORD will deliver us.' Has any of the
gods of the nations delivered his land out of the hand of the king of
Assyria? Where are the gods of Hamath and Arpad? Where are the

10. Radner, *Ancient Assyria*, 16.

gods of Sepharvaim? Have they delivered Samaria out of my hand? Who among all the gods of these lands have delivered their lands out of my hand, that the LORD should deliver Jerusalem out of my hand?" (36:18–20). It is, thus, clear that the Rabshakeh and Sennacherib view Yahweh as but one of many patron deities of weaker nations. Notably, even though Sennacherib considers the patron deities of conquered nations inferior, he nevertheless affirms the reality of their existence. At one point he even seeks sends priests back into the territory of the vanquished northern kingdom of Israel so as to appease the "god of the land" (cf. 2 Kgs 17:26–27).

King Hezekiah, however, rightfully acknowledges that the LORD belongs to a different category than the gods of the nations. In prayerful humility, the king makes petitions to the "God of Israel," while still acknowledging that Yahweh is the maker of heaven and earth and the God of "all kingdoms of the earth" (37:16).

Yahweh hears the prayer of King Hezekiah. He declares that he will fight on behalf of his people (37:21–35). As a result, two things happen. Firstly, the angel of the LORD goes out and strikes down 185,000 soldiers in the camp of the Assyrians, causing the remainder of the army to retreat in fear (37:36). Secondly, God defeats the Assyrian king in his hometown: "Then Sennacherib king of Assyria departed and returned home and lived at Nineveh. And as he was worshiping in the house of Nisroch his god, Adrammelech and Sharezer, his sons, struck him down with the sword. And after they escaped into the land of Ararat, Esarhaddon his son reigned in his place" (37:37–38). While the exact identity of Nisroch is unknown, and the subject of no little debate, it is likely that the name is an epithet of one of the known Assyrian gods. One possible identity is none other than the god Ashur himself.[11]

In an example of perfect dramatic irony, King Hezekiah humbly goes to the temple of the true God and is delivered, whereas King Sennacherib proudly goes to the temple of his false god and is murdered. For while Sennacherib possessed exponentially more power than Hezekiah, the cosmic perspective on Isaiah 36—37 reveals that Yahweh is infinitely more powerful than Ashur.

11. See: Grayson, "Nisroch (Deity)." In *AYBD* 1122.

A GRECO-ROMAN SPIRIT COSMOLOGY

A final consideration regarding the conceptual backgrounds behind Paul's understanding of powers relates to the spirit cosmology of the Greco-Roman world; a world in which Paul and his readers lived. While Greco-Roman views of spiritual reality would have differed from that of the Old Testament in a variety of significant ways, there are, nevertheless, remarkable aspects in which ancient pagan sources parallel the "Deuteronomy 32 worldview." For example, in *Critias*, Plato even explicitly refers to geographical allotments being disturbed among various gods:

> In the days of old, the gods had the whole earth distributed among them by allotment. There was not quarrelling; for you cannot rightly suppose that the gods did not know what was proper for each of them to have, or, knowing this, they would seek to procure for themselves by contention that which properly belonged to others. They all of them by just appointment obtained what they wanted, and peopled their own districts; and when they had peopled them they tended us, their nurslings and possessions, as shepherds tend their flocks, excepting that they did not use blows or bodily force, as shepherds do, but governed us like pilots from the stern of the vessel, which is an easy way of guiding animals, holding our souls by the rudder of persuasion according to their pleasure;—thus did they guide all mortal creatures.[12]

This example shows how not only the existence of spiritual beings but even how ideas akin to "cosmic geography" could fit within the purview of Greek philosophy. As Ghanan theologian Daniel K. Darko notes, "Unlike our post-enlightenment prisms, critical thinking and spirituality belong together. To believe in the reality of supernatural powers to influence human thoughts and praxis was not akin to ignorance in Greek philosophy, which would ultimately form the foundations of western intellectual tradition."[13]

12. Plato, *Critias*, 109.

13. Darko, *Against Powers and Principalities*, 24.

For first-century societies of Mediterranean Europe, gods and goddesses presided over all human life and influenced the success and failure of both individuals and communities. Polytheism was normative, whereas the monotheism of Judaism and Christianity was seen as outlier. The Greco-Roman gods played a key role in the communal identity of cities and nations. As such, faithful worship of these gods was part of the culture and well-being of Greco-Roman society.[14] In fact, most Greek cities hosted a patron deity, whose regular worship was considered a civic duty. Participation in cultic festivals of such divine patrons was a culturally expected act of national loyalty, in which politics and piety were seen as inseparable realities.[15]

While some authors have posited that Paul's conception of powers derives primarily from Greek philosophical sources as opposed to that of Jewish apocalyptic literature,[16] such a view is neither necessary nor persuasive. After all, in describing the powers and Christ's supremacy over the powers, Paul does not appeal to Plato, Philo, or Plutarch. He does appeal to cosmically oriented Old Testament passages.

Nevertheless, what is beyond dispute is that ideas coming from a "Deuteronomy 32 worldview" would have been thoroughly comprehensible within the framework of Greco-Roman spirit cosmology. Thus, while Paul would have written from a perspective primarily formed by the Old Testament and Second Temple Jewish thought, his ideas, and even his terminology, concerning spiritual beings and the relationship of spiritual beings to people groups and geographic territories would have been highly intelligible to gentile residents of Asia Minor, Greece, and the Italian peninsula (i.e., the gentile readers of his epistles).

---

14. Darko, *Against Powers and Principalities*, 21.

15. Darko, *Against Powers and Principalities*, 31–34.

16. See: Forbes, "Pauline Demonology and/or Cosmology? Principalities, Powers and the Elements of the World in Their Hellenistic Context," 51–73.

7

THE DIVINE WARRIOR

THE LORD IS A MAN OF WAR

As the gods of the nations are often depicted as adversaries of God and his people, the Old Testament consistently characterizes the LORD as a divine warrior who fights on behalf of his people and overwhelmingly defeats all rival forces. Perhaps the most famous instance of this characterization occurs in the "Song of Moses" of Exodus 15, which immediately follows the defeat of Pharaoh and the Egyptian armies at the Red Sea. Here, Moses declares, "The LORD is a man of war; the LORD is his name" (Exod 15:3). While the Egyptian armies come to fight against the people of Israel, it is Yahweh who goes to war with them, "Pharaoh's chariots and his host he cast into the sea, and his chosen officers were sunk in the Red Sea. The floods covered them; they went down into the depths like a stone. Your right hand, O LORD, glorious in power, your right hand, O LORD, shatters the enemy" (15:4–6). Yet, it would be a mistake to view this contest merely as battle between a deity and the martial forces of man. According to Egyptian religion, Pharaoh was the incarnation of the god Horus and the image of the god Ra.[1] For both the Egyptians and the Israelites, such a victory represented nothing less than the God of Israel prevailing over the

---

1. Frankfurt, *Kingship and the Gods*, 149.

chief god of Egypt. For this reason, the "Song of Moses" explicitly declares: "Who is like you, O LORD, *among the gods*? Who is like you, majestic in holiness, awesome in glorious deeds, doing wonders? You stretched out your right hand; the earth swallowed them" (15:11–12; emphasis added).

In understanding this divine warrior motif, it is important to understand the ways that the LORD is both like and dislike the patron powers of the nations. The similarity lies in the fact that Yahweh is indeed a spiritual being who claims a nation (Israel) as his "allotted heritage" (Deut 32:9). However, in addition to the creator/creation distinction previously mentioned, the LORD is unwilling to be coerced or manipulated by his people. Unlike, the relationship between the Moabite King Mesha and his patron god Chemosh (2 Kgs 3:26–27), the God of Israel's power will not be co-opted for the agenda of any nation or leader of a nation. This is evident in Joshua's encounter with Yahweh in Joshua 5.[2] When Joshua asks the man with a drawn sword whether he is on the side of Israel or Jericho, God bluntly answers, "No; but I am the commander of the army of the LORD. Now I have come" (Josh 5:14a). The LORD is a warrior, but he is not a mercenary.

This holy independence of Yahweh is also reflected in the "Ark Narrative" of 1 Samuel, which recounts how the ark was once at home in the tabernacle of Shiloh (1 Sam 4:3–4), how it was captured by the Philistines in a battle and taken to the temple of Dagon (the national patron god of Philistia)[3] as a trophy (4:11—5:12; cf. Judg 16:23), and how it was eventually returned to Israel (6:1—7:2). The narrative shows the ark is not a magical object that may be wielded to manipulate the LORD. When Eli's evil sons take the ark into battle against the Philistines as if it were a nationalist mascot, God judges their insolence with death and destruction (4:3–4,10–11). Nevertheless, Yahweh's decapitation of Dagon's idol and subsequent defeat of the Philistines illustrate how the God of

---

2. For arguments to why the figure of Joshua 5:13–14 is Yahweh and not an angel see: Howard, *Joshua*, 157.

3. Block, *The Gods of the Nations*, 39.

Israel is a fierce warrior king who does not require an army to win his battles (5:1–9).

God is for his own agenda. That agenda, moreover, cannot be reduced to a mere promoting of the Israelite nation and opposition of the gentile nations. Indeed, multiple passages with the divine warrior motif connect Yahweh's martial activity to the *redemption* of the nations. Particularly important to Paul's understanding of powers, are the passages of Psalm 2, Psalm 68, Isaiah 59—60, and Daniel 7.

PSALM 2

"Why do the nations rage?" the Psalmist asks (Ps 2:1a). Why do the peoples "plot" (*yehgu*) rebellion in the same way that the blessed man of Psalm 1 "meditates" (*yehgeh*) on the law of the LORD (2:1b)? The answer given is that the "kings" and "rulers" of the earth have conspired together against the LORD and his "Anointed" messiah (*meshih*) in order to break the bonds and cast away the cords of divine authority (2:2–3). They aspire to self-determination and autonomy, independent from any external influence, including that of God himself.[4]

While it is possible to see the "kings" and "rulers" of verse 2 as synonyms, the Greek Septuagint translates "rulers" (Heb. *rozenim*) as "*archontes*" a term which Paul uses to convey spiritual powers in 1 Corinthians 2:6, 8 and Ephesians 2:2.[5] This implies a cosmic dimension to the psalm, wherein both gentile human rulers and spiritual powers both desire independence from the reign of God.[6] Psalm 2 is, thus, an image of cosmic insurrection and spiritual warfare.

---

4. Note that terms like "autonomy," "independence," and "self-determination" are also often explicitly designated as virtues by advocates of nationalism.

5. Other New Testament references where "ruler/prince" (*archōn*) refers to Satan or demonic powers include: Matt 9:34, 12:24, (potentially 20:25); Mark 3:22; Luke 11:15; John 12:31; 14:30; 16:11.

6. "The hostile powers want to be autonomous, independent of Yahweh and the one who represents his lordship." Kraus, *A Continental Commentary*, 128.

But the LORD mocks the futility of this rebellion (2:4). For the true begotten Son has been imbued with sovereign power and authority (2:7), and as the messianic warrior "king" (2:6), he will break the power of his enemies "with a rod of iron and dash them in pieces like a potter's vessel" (2:9). The Son will receive the "inheritance" (*nahalath*) of the "nations" (*goyim*) (2:8),[7] which, by implication, has been seized from the rulers. The kings are called to be wise and rulers are warned: serve, worship, take refuge in the Son, or else endure his wrath (2:10–12). Thus, Psalm 2 begins with the rebellion of the nations but concludes with God's reclamation of the nations.

PSALM 68

Psalm 68 begins with an image of Yahweh as the divine warrior who "shall arise" (*yaqum*)[8] to defeat his enemies (Ps 68:1). Before the infinite power of God, the wicked flee, and the righteous rejoice (68:2–3). Scholars have connected this psalm to the procession of the Ark of the Covenant to Jerusalem under the reign of David (cf. 2 Sam 6).[9] As a whole, then, the psalm functions as a picture of the enthronement of the LORD as king.

The text is filled with a vision of dramatic reversal and re-definition: God becomes a father to the fatherless, a protector of widows, and a liberator of prisoners, while exiling the rebellious to a parched land (68:5–6). The earth quakes before the might of the God of Sinai, who commands the forces of nature (68:7–10). Before such a divine warrior, the courage of enemy kings melts like snow, and they flee before his power (68:11–14).

The taunt to the many peaked mountains of Bashan in verse 15 may indicate that the conflict in Psalm 68 is of a spiritual nature.

---

7. Both "inheritance" (*nahalath*) of the "nations" (*goyim*) are also key terms in Deuteronomy 32:8.

8. Here, like Psalm 82, the term "arise" (*qumi*) provides a conceptual link between the doctrines of Christ's resurrection and ascension and Yahweh's reclamation of the nations.

9. Kidner, *Psalms 1–72*, 256.

Bashan most likely refers to Mount Hermon, which is the tallest mountain in Israel. Sources of the Second Temple period and ancient Near East literature respectively connect Hermon with demonic spirits[10] and pagan gods.[11] Rather than the proud mountain of the false gods of the nations, Yahweh has chosen humble Zion to be his dwelling place (68:16). As the LORD ascends his throne in victory, a train of captives, taken as spoils from the defeated gods, follows him: "You ascended on high, leading a host of captives in your train and receiving gifts among men, even among the rebellious, that the LORD God may dwell there" (68:18).

This train of captives, which Paul later quotes in Ephesians 4:8, shifts to an image of a victory parade with representative of the various tribes of Israel (68:24–27). However, the blessings of God's reign extend beyond the Israelite nation: "Because of your temple at Jerusalem kings shall bear gifts to you . . . Nobles shall come from Egypt; Cush shall hasten to stretch out her hands to God" (68:29, 31). While defeated enemies are often required to bring tribute to their sovereign, the rest of the psalm indicates that the gifts of the gentile nations represent freewill offerings of doxology and devotion, rather than begrudging duty: "O kingdoms of the earth, sing to God; sing praises to the LORD, to him who rides in the heavens, the ancient heavens; behold, he sends out his voice, his mighty voice" (68:32–33). Yet again, as a result of his victory over enemy gods, the peoples of the nations are reclaimed as a part of the people of God.

ISAIAH 59—60

The oracles of Isaiah 59 focus on the Yahweh's righteous indignation toward injustice: "Justice is turned back, and righteousness stands far away; for truth has stumbled in the public squares, and uprightness cannot enter. Truth is lacking, and he who departs from evil makes himself a prey. The LORD saw it, and it displeased

10. Olson, "1 Enoch." In *Eerdmans Commentary on the Bible* 908.
11. Arav, "Hermon, Mount (Place)." In *AYBD* 158.

him that there was no justice" (Isa 59:14–15). The LORD sees the powers of evil and oppression and the havoc they have wrought upon his people and his creation at large. In such a vicious world, even the one who departs from evil becomes prey to those who lie in wait for blood. Yet, the God of Israel will not passively allow such wickedness to endure forever:

> He saw that there was no man, and wondered that there was no one to intercede; then his own arm brought him salvation, and his righteousness upheld him. He put on righteousness as a breastplate, and a helmet of salvation on his head; he put on garments of vengeance for clothing, and wrapped himself in zeal as a cloak. According to their deeds, so will he repay, wrath to his adversaries, repayment to his enemies; to the coastlands he will render repayment. So they shall fear the name of the LORD from the west, and his glory from the rising of the sun; for he will come like a rushing stream, which the wind of the LORD drives (Isa 59:16–19).

It is not difficult to surmise the importance of Isaiah 59:16–19 regarding Paul's thought on powers. The vision of Yahweh's armor in verse 17 forms the prototype image of Paul's "armor of God" in Ephesians 6:13–17. Thus, Paul clearly interprets Isaiah 59 as referring to warfare on a cosmic and spiritual level.

Interestingly, Isaiah 59 shows that the fierce power of the divine warrior will also have an effect on the nations beyond Israel. The LORD will repay his adversaries according to their deeds with his wrath (59:18). But the text also seems to imply that those who dwell from the east (the rising of the sun) to the west and the coastlands, will come to fear the LORD (59:19). In other words, because of Yahweh's victory, there will be members of the gentile nations who experience God's judgment, but there will also be members of the gentile nations who will experience God's salvation.

Not coincidentally, the following chapter of Isaiah 60 confirms the LORD's plan of redemption for the nations. Immediately following the divine warrior image of Isaiah 59, the first word of Isaiah 60 is "arise" (qumi), which as we have seen is a word connected to the victory of God over spiritual powers resulting in the reclamation of the nations for himself (cf. Pss 68:1; 82:8). Here, that link is reaffirmed: "And nations shall come to your light, and kings to the brightness of your rising" (60:3). People from former enemy nations like "Midian" shall bring gifts of worship to the Holy City. Even ships from "Tarshish," representing the ends of the earth, shall come to worship the God of Israel.

Moreover, this vision indicates a redemptive reversal of cosmic proportions. Earlier in the book of Isaiah, images like the "ships of Tarshish" and the "cedars of Lebanon" once functioned as symbols of fallen, idolatrous human culture produced by pagan nations (cf. 2:12–18). There, they are portrayed as objects of God's just wrath. But now in chapter 60, they are objects of God's redemption. Thus, with these images Isaiah seems to imagine, more than just a restoration of Israel. He is witnessing what a fully redeemed culture from all nations might look like. Commenting on this passage, theologian Richard Mouw writes:

> God will stand in judgment of all idolatrous and prideful attachments to military, technological, commercial, and cultural might. He will destroy all of those rebellious projects that glorify oppression, exploitation, and accumulation of possessions. It is in such projects that we can discern our own ships of Tarshish and cedars from Lebanon. But the 'stuff' of human culture will nonetheless be gathered into the Holy City . . . . The earth—including the American military and French art and Chinese medicine and Nigerian agriculture—belongs to the Lord. And he will reclaim all of these things, harnessing them for service in the City.[12]

So great and comprehensive is the victory of God that even the descendants of those who had oppressed the Jewish people will have a place in the city of God: "The sons of those who afflicted you shall come bending low to you, and all who despised you shall bow down at your feet; they shall call you the City of the LORD, the Zion of the Holy One of Israel" (60:14). Thus, in Isaiah's mind, the

w, *When the Kings Come Marching*, 39.

heavenly city becomes a reversal of the tower of Babel in Genesis 11. At Babel, men were united in rebellion against God. In the city of the LORD, men will be united in the worship of God. At Babel, man sought to work his way to God. In the city of the LORD, God graciously comes down to man. At Babel, the nations were scattered in judgment. In the city of the LORD, the nations will be gathered for salvation, for the light of the LORD will radiate a magnetic beauty that will call the nations to worship the living God.

DANIEL 7

Finally, Daniel 7 comprises an apocalyptic vision of cosmic and spiritual warfare. In this vision, various beasts war with one another for dominion and authority over the earth (Dan 7:1–8). In alignment with Deuteronomy 32:8, these beasts seem to represent the spiritual forces that stand behind the pagan nations of the earth. Eventually, the LORD, as the "Ancient of Days," definitively defeats the final beast, and the dominion of all beasts of the earth is reclaimed (7:9 12). Yahweh then delegates this authority to a divine figure called the "Son of Man," signifying a restoration of humankind's dominion that was lost in the fall of man (7:13–14). This Son of Man is the one anointed by Yahweh to bring forth ultimate judgment and justice to the nations of world.

In the Septuagint rendering of this passage, there is a lexical link between the "authority" (*exousia*) taken away from the beasts of the earth and the "authority" (*exousia*) of spiritual powers in the book of Ephesians (LXX Dan 7:14; Eph 1:21; 2:2; 6:12). Thus, for Paul, Daniel's vision prefigures the moment in which God definitively defeats the various powers of evil and reclaims dominion over all creation. Though the spiritual forces behind the empires of men—like Babylon in the time of Daniel and Rome in the time of Paul—would have seemed invincible in their day, God declares that his authority is far greater. Thus, Daniel 7 anticipates Paul's conception of Christ, who definitively defeats the power of evil and reigns in victory.

SUMMARY OF PART II

In sum, the Old Testament, Second Temple period literature, and ancient Near East sources build a picture of spiritual reality that form the background to the Apostle Paul's understanding of the powers, the nations, and the spiritual relationship between the powers and the nations. Scholars have referred to this perspective as "cosmic geography" or the "Deuteronomy 32 worldview." Moreover, the strong association with this view and Paul's notion of the powers is established by multiple lexical links and conceptual connections.

According to this "Deuteronomy 32 worldview," God allotted spiritual dominion over the gentile nations to the "sons of God" at Babel, but he chose Israel as his own portion (Deut 32:8–9). These "sons of God" seem to be equivalent to spiritual beings who are members of God's divine council (Ps 82) and patron angels over nations, who are often worshipped as gods (Isa 36:18–20; Dan 10:13, 20). As a result of this allotment, gentile nations have suffered injustice and spiritual blindness at the hands of these false "gods." While this spirit cosmology bears a distinctively Jewish flavor, parallels with Greco-Roman religion and philosophy show that such a view of spiritual reality would have been highly comprehensible to the gentile readers of Paul's letters.

Finally, as the mighty divine warrior, the Old Testament testifies to a day when Yahweh will "arise" to defeat the wayward "sons of God" and reclaim the nations for himself (Pss 2, 68; Isa 59:14—60:22; Dan 7:13–14). Indeed, the next section will explore how Paul applied "Deuteronomy 32 worldview" to his understanding of the powers, as well as how the reign of the powers found their end in the life, death, resurrection, and ascension of Jesus Christ of Nazareth.

Part III

THE APOSTLE, THE POWERS, AND THE NATIONS

8

THE COURSE OF THIS WORLD

THE APOSTLE TO THE NATIONS

Ananias marveled that the Lord would command him to seek out and pray for Saul of Tarsus. He had heard the stories of this religious fanatic who imagined himself Phinehas reborn; breathing threats and murder, burning with zeal. In fact, Saul had come to Ananias's hometown of Damascus for the express purpose of arresting and extraditing those who worshipped Jesus of Nazareth as Lord and God. However, the Lord had a plan for Saul: "But the Lord said to [Ananias], 'Go, for he is a chosen instrument of mine to carry my name before the Gentiles (*ethōn*) and kings and the children of Israel. For I will show him how much he must suffer for the sake of my name'" (Acts 9:15–16). Saul the Pharisee will become known as Paul—the Apostle to the gentiles.

In his letter to the churches that he planted in Galatia, Paul explicitly acknowledges a self-awareness that he had been set apart before birth, called by grace, and saved through the revelation of Son of God, so that he "might preach the [Christ] among the Gentiles" (Gal 1:15–16). This internal sense of calling was later externally confirmed by the Apostles James, Cephas (i.e., Peter), and John, who acknowledged that Paul "had been entrusted with the gospel to the uncircumcised" (2:7–9). Central to this gospel was the doctrine that the gentiles shall be justified by faith. Moreover, far from a novel departure from Jewish orthodoxy, Paul understands the gentile inclusion into God's people as the fulfillment of God's ancient promise Abraham: "Know then that it is those of faith who are the sons of Abraham. And the Scripture, foreseeing that God would justify the Gentiles (*ethnē*) by faith, preached the gospel beforehand to Abraham, saying, 'In you shall all the nations (*ethnē*) be blessed.' So then, those who are of faith are blessed along with Abraham, the man of faith" (3:7–9).

In his letter to the Romans, Paul echoes this same logic. He states Christ's saving work confirms God's faithfulness to "the promises given to the patriarchs, and in order that the Gentiles might glorify God for his mercy" (Rom 15:8–9). Paul anchors God's plan to redeem people from gentile nations to a wide array of Old Testament passages, appealing to samples from the Torah, Prophets, and Writings (Rom 15:9–1 2; 2 Sam 22:50; Ps 18:49; Deut 32:43; Ps 117:1; Isa 11:1).[1] More than a generic theology of mission, Paul seems to have personalized the call for the people of God to bring the gentiles to faith and obedience. As a divinely commissioned apostle to the nations, Paul has been granted grace " . . . to be a minister of Christ Jesus to the Gentiles in the priestly service of the gospel of God, so that the offering of the Gentiles may be acceptable, sanctified by the Holy Spirit" (Rom 15:16). For this reason, Paul desires to come to Rome so that the Roman church might support him into pressing further west into territories where Christ has yet to be named (15:20–28).

To the nations, Paul has been sent; and to the nations, he will go. In Acts, Luke recounts three of Paul's missionary journeys in which he plants churches in the gentile territories of Cyprus, Asia Minor, Macedonia, and Greece. During the second missionary journey, Paul comes to Athens, where he delivers a famous address to the public intellectuals of the Areopagus. Among other topics and ideas, this speech includes insight into Paul's understanding of nations: "And he made from one man every nation of mankind to

---

1. Given the prior section on backgrounds, it is not insignificant that Paul connects the redemption of the gentiles to Deuteronomy 32.

live on all the face of the earth, having determined allotted periods and the boundaries of their dwelling place, that they should seek God, and perhaps feel their way toward him and find him. Yet he is actually not far from each one of us" (Acts 17:26–27). Here, Paul expresses an understanding of nations as distinct people groups who share a common humanity. Paul attributes the diversity of nations to the providence of God, as opposed to the contingent events of history. Each nation possesses a unique role in time and space; in history and on the globe. Moreover, the reference to allotted "boundaries" (*horothesias*) indicates that Paul views the nations through the prism of Deuteronomy 32:8: "When the Most High distributed nations as he scattered the descendants of Adam, he set up boundaries (*horia*) for the nations according to the number of the angels of God" (Deut 32:8, *LES*).[2]

WHAT THE POWERS DO AND HOW THEY RELATE TO THE NATIONS

Not only does Paul understand the nations in light of Deuteronomy 32, but his understanding of the spiritual powers seems to have this worldview in the background as well. As already mentioned in chapter 2, Paul's preferred word-choice in describing evil spirits suggests that such spirits possess authority and dominion over territories and people groups. Thus, it is not without warrant to deduce a connection between the "sons of God/angels" of Deuteronomy 32:8 and "rulers" (*archē*), "authorities" (*exousias*), "powers" (*dynamis*), "dominions" (*kyriotēs*), "thrones" (*thronos*), and "cosmic powers" (*kosmokratōr*) of Pauline thought.[3]

In Romans 8, the powers are listed among obstructions that apparently actively seek to separate God's people from God's love:

2. Both conservative and critical scholars have observed a connection between Acts 17:26 and Deuteronomy 32:8. See: Marshall, *Acts*, 304 and Pervo, *Acts*, 436.

3. As the previous chapters have noted, Paul's terms for the powers also form numerous lexical connections with LXX Old Testament passages related to territorial spirits.

"For I am sure that neither death nor life, nor angels nor rulers, nor things present nor things to come, nor powers, nor height nor depth, nor anything else in all creation, will be able to separate us from the love of God in Christ Jesus our Lord" (Rom 8:38–39). Here, "angels" (*angeloi*) and "rulers" (*archai*) indicate evil spiritual beings that stand in opposition to God. Moreover, it is possible that these spiritual forces may stand behind the physical realities listed in 8:35 (i.e., tribulation, distress, persecution, famine, nakedness, danger, and sword). Paul's similar use of "rulers (*archontōn*) of this age"[4] in 1 Corinthians 2:6–8 explicitly connects such spiritual powers with civic means of persecution and execution, since they are credited with "[having crucified] the Lord of glory."[5]

In addition to seeing the powers at work through physical means, such as state governments, Paul envisions the powers holding people in spiritual captivity, resulting in spiritual blindness: "In their case the god of this world has blinded the minds of the unbelievers, to keep them from seeing the light of the gospel of the glory of Christ, who is the image of God" (2 Cor 4:4). In this context, "the god of this world" almost certainly refers to Satan as the chief prince of other evil spirits (cf. Matt 12:24; John 12:31, 14:30, 16:11).[6] How did Satan acquire spiritual rulership over the world? Michael S. Heiser postulates that Paul's word choice in characterizing Satan as the "god of this world" may reflect a wordplay on Satan being cast down to the earth at the time of the fall (Isa 14:12–5 l; Ezek 28:11–19; Gen 3).[7] So, while man abdicated his

4. While not all scholars view this term as referencing spiritual beings, understanding the "rulers" as "angelic custodians of nations" is one of the major veins of interpretation. For an extensive overview of the term "rulers of this age" see: Thiselton, *The First Epistle to the Corinthians*, 233–239.

5. For the early Christians whose loyalty to Jesus was viewed by the empire as disloyalty to Caesar and the Roman nation, persecution at the hands of the state was thus viewed as not only physical but also spiritual opposition. As Justin Martyr wrote in his *Second Apology*, " . . . the evil demons, who hate us, and who keep such men as these subject to themselves, and serving them in the capacity of judges, incite them, as rulers actuated by evil spirits, to put us [Christians] to death." Justin Martyr, "The Second Apology of Justin," ch. 1.

6. Garland, *2 Corinthians*, 210–212.

7. Heiser, *Demons*, 81.

divinely apportioned dominion over the earth in rebelling against God (cf. Gen 1:28; 3:17), Satan laid claim to it, thus becoming "the god of this world." To be under the rule of Satan and the powers is to be imprisoned in a "domain of darkness" (Col 1:13). This is why, in Ephesians, Paul equates such spiritual subjugation to spiritual death: "And you were dead in the trespasses and sins in which you once walked, following the course of this world, following the prince of the power of the air, the spirit that is now at work in the sons of disobedience—among whom we all once lived in the passions of our flesh, carrying out the desires of the body and the mind, and were by nature children of wrath, like the rest of mankind" (Eph 2:1–3).

Paul, thus, understands human life outside of Christ as being under the spiritual dominion of hostile spiritual forces that oppose the rule of God. This spiritual condition is rendered and referred to as "this world" (2:2) and "this age" (1:21). Thus, the "world" is not a spatial term—it is the demonic domain of fractured creation and fallen humanity, ruled by the powers (Rom 8:38; 1 Cor 15:24; Col 2:14).[8] Such is the inescapable condition of all men, both Jew and gentile.

However, the state of spiritual subjugation and death in Ephesians 2:1 is coordinated with ethnic separation and hostility in Ephesians 2:12. For Paul, "You were dead in trespasses . . . following the course of this world, following the prince of the power of the air" (2:1) is directly parallel to "you were at that time separated from Christ, alienated from the commonwealth of Israel . . . without God in the world" (2:12). While the condition of spiritual death and darkness via the dominion of the powers is universal to all who are outside of Christ, Paul also sees the powers playing a role in cultivating communal identities among people of various cultures. The powers captivate people groups within the bounds of their nationality and ethnicity through the means of what Paul calls "*stoichea*"; a term that Paul uses only in conjunction with the powers. Translated as "elemental spirits" (*ESV*), "spiritual forces" (*NIV*), or "elemental principles" (*NASB*), *stoichea* is a difficult

---

8. Ridderbos, *Paul*, 91.

term to define. In *Delivered from The Elements of the World*, Peter J. Leithart suggests that Paul sees the *stoicheia* as socio-religious practices, structures, and symbols that organize fallen human life outside of Christ for both Jew and Gentile alike.[9]

Note the relationship between the "elemental spirits of the world" and the "rulers and authorities" in the following passage from Colossians 2:

> See to it that no one takes you captive by philosophy and empty deceit, according to human tradition, according to the elemental spirits (*stoichea*) of the world, and not according to Christ. . . . He disarmed the rulers (*archas*) and authorities (*exousias*) and put them to open shame, by triumphing over them in him. Therefore let no one pass judgment on you in questions of food and drink, or with regard to a festival or a new moon or a Sabbath. . . . If with Christ you died to the elemental spirits (*stoicheōn*) of the world, why, as if you were still alive in the world, do you submit to regulations— "Do not handle, Do not taste, Do not touch" (referring to things that all perish as they are used)—according to human precepts and teachings? These have indeed an appearance of wisdom in promoting self-made religion and asceticism and severity to the body, but they are of no value in stopping the indulgence of the flesh (Col 2:8, 15–16; 20–23).

Here, the "elemental principles" (*stoicheōn*) seem to rule over human life for those who have not been united to Christ. As Hendrik Berkhof notes, "They are manifested in human traditions [and] in public opinion which threatens to entice the Christians in Colossae away from Christ."[10]

The only other place where Paul uses the term "elemental principles" (*stoicheōn*) is in Galatians 4:

> In the same way we also, when we were children, were enslaved to the elementary principles (*stoicheōn*) of the world . . . . Formerly, when you did not know God, you

9. Leithart, *Delivered from the Elements of the World*, 26.
10. Berkhof, *Christ and the Powers*, 20.

were enslaved to those that by nature are not gods. But now that you have come to know God, or rather to be known by God, how can you turn back again to the weak and worthless elementary principles (*stoicheōn*) of the world, whose slaves you want to be once more? You observe days and months and seasons and years! I am afraid I may have labored over you in vain (Gal 4:3; 8–11).

The subject matter bears a striking resemblance to the Apostle's line of thought in Colossians. In both cases, Paul admonishes Christians against allowing either gentile or Jewish cultural norms, expectations, or identities to claim dominion over their lives. Fascinatingly, Paul sees allegiance to ethnic/national identity as something through which the powers seek to oppose the claims of Jesus's absolute lordship. To be sure, Paul does not consider ethnic identity itself as inherently negative or sinful, for God himself made the nations (cf. Acts 17:26). However, for those baptized into Christ, ethnicity must no longer determine one's ultimate identity (Gal 3:28; Col 3:11). To relapse into an unhealthy, idolatrous relationship with national identity is akin to being "enslaved to elementary principles of this world" and "self-made religion" (Gal 4:3, 8–11; Col 2:23).

The *stoichea* are, thus, wielded by the powers to enslave the nations within the socio-religious bondage of their ethnic and cultural allegiance. The powers instrumentalize symbols, structures, and cultural pressures to cultivate nationalistic pride that is inherently contrary to life in Christ.[11] Astonishingly, the powers can even weaponize the *stoichea* to lure even those who are already "alive in Christ" (Col 2:13, 20) to live within a fleshly allegiance to old nationalistic loyalties.

In sum, the powers seek to separate God's people from God's love. They work in and through institutions and societal structures, like the state, to violently oppose and oppress the people and

---

11. I will explore specific historical and contemporary examples of how the powers have utilized such "symbols, structures, and cultural pressures" to cultivate nationalism in Part IV of the present volume.

purposes of God on the earth. They possess a spiritual dominion over the fallen world and life outside of Christ, which results in alienation from God and cultural hostility and division among nations of the world. They enslave people with a spiritual allegiance to cultural traditions that are interwoven with ethnic/national identity, and can even tempt the people of God toward relapsing into spiritual bondage unto the "elemental principles (*stoicheōn*)of this world." Moreover, Paul's conception of nations and spiritual powers that rule over the nations seems to flow organically from the Old Testament, namely from what has been called "cosmic geography" or the "Deuteronomy 32 worldview."

Given this analysis, there is sufficient biblical rationale to show that there is (and always has been) a spiritual agency behind what we term as nationalism in the contemporary era. If nationalism is the exaltation of a nation or conception of a nation to a place of highest allegiance, concern, and devotion, wherein love for one's nation is "a paramount, a supreme loyalty, commanding all others,"[12] it should be clear by now that Paul would understand such a phenomenon not only as idolatrous, but as being propagated by spiritual powers who stand in opposition to God and his people. While not all powers necessarily have exclusively nationalistic aims, nationalism—in all of its variegated forms—has always been related to the powers. Over against the seductive siren calls of such powers, the people of God are to embrace true freedom in the far greater power of Christ Jesus (Gal 5:1).

12. Hayes, *Nationalism*,10.

9

THE POWER OF GOD
OVER THE POWERS OF DARKNESS

THE GREATER POWER OF CHRIST

While Paul clearly envisions the powers as entities that pose an intimidating spiritual threat, he does not place them on the same level of being or authority as that of God the Lord. Though spiritual, the powers belong to the category of "creation" (Rom 8:38–39). Christ, who is "the visible image of the invisible God," is to be held as preeminent over the powers: "For by him all things were created, in heaven and on earth, visible and invisible, whether thrones (*thronoi*) or dominions (*kyriotētes*) or rulers (*archai*) or authorities (*exousiai*)—all things were created through him and for him" (Col 1:15–16). While powerful, the "rulers (*archotōn*) of this age" do not possess the divine attribute of omnipotence, for their reign is "doomed to pass away" (1 Cor 2:6). While possessing intelligence, the "rulers" are not omniscient, for if they were, they would not have sealed their own downfall by "[crucifying] the Lord of glory" (2:8). Thus, Paul wants his readers to know that the powers are real and the powers are dangerous. Yet, because of the victory of Christ, the powers are also doomed.

The contrast between the powers of darkness and the far greater power of God is a recurring motif that flows through many of the Pauline epistles.[1] Against the "powers" (*dynameis*) that would seek to separate God from his people (Rom 8:38), the "gospel . . . is the power (*dynamis*) of God for salvation to everyone who believes, to the Jew first and also to the Greek" (Rom 1:16). Over against worldly power and wisdom, "Christ crucified" is "the power (*dynamin*) of God and the wisdom of God" (1 Cor 1:23–24). Christ is "the head of all rule (*archēs*) and authority (*exousias*)" (Col 2:10) through whom God "disarmed the rulers (*archas*) and authorities (*exousias*) and put them to open shame" (2:15).

Christ is supreme over the powers, for the powers owe their very existence to him, as the one for whom and through him all things were created (Col 1:16–17). However, the supremacy of Christ is not only displayed in the work of creation, but particularly in the work of redemption. Christ has died, and Christ is risen. Death, the ultimate weapon of the powers and the veil that was once spread over the nations, has been overcome and swallowed up in the triumph of Christ's resurrection (cf. Isa 25:7–8).

Moreover, as the ascended king, Christ has taken that which once belonged to the powers through cosmic conquest. The Lord has bound and disarmed the strong man so that he may plunder his goods (cf. Matt 12:29). This is why the powers are now pow*erless* to separate God's people from God's love: "Who is to condemn? Christ Jesus is the one who died—more than that, who was raised—who is at the right hand of God, who indeed is interceding for us" (Rom 8:34). Christ's resurrection is the firstfruits of the final and ultimate resurrection, which spells the final destruction of " . . . every rule (*archēn*) and every authority (*exsousian*) and power (*dynamin*)," including the "last enemy," which is "death" (1 Cor 15:20, 24, 26).

---

1. Many contemporary biblical scholars deny Pauline authorship of all thirteen epistles that are attributed to him in the New Testament. As it is well beyond the scope of this book, I feel it is unnecessary to argue my views here concerning the authorship of the disputed Pauline letters. Interestingly, however, it is worthwhile to note that the theme of "power" appears in almost all of the canonical books attributed to Paul, whether they are disputed or not.

But even now, as the ascended king of heaven, Jesus is already seated in the heavenly places, above all other powers (Eph 1:20–21). Even more, those who have been united to Christ have been seated with him in the heavenly places, so that they too might share in Christ's victory over the powers (Eph 1:3).

THE THEME OF POWER IN EPHESIANS

While several Pauline epistles emphasize the power of God over the powers of darkness, this contrast becomes a dominant theme in Paul's letter to the Ephesians. The Apostle introduces this idea in the first chapter by juxtaposing the "immeasurable greatness of his [Christ's] power" (Eph 1:19) with "all rule and authority and power and dominion" of spiritual darkness (Eph 1:21).

The "immeasurable greatness of his power" (Eph 1:19) clearly refers to the absolutely supreme power of God the Father and the Lord Jesus Christ. This power specifically relates to the power that God the Father " . . . worked in Christ when he raised him from the dead and seated him at his right hand in the heavenly places" (Eph 1:20). However, the power of God refers not only to Christ's resurrection but also to Christ's ascension to the "right hand" of God. This later aspect of Christ's exaltation bears particular importance on the relationship of the power of God to the powers of evil. Because Christ is seated at the right hand of God, he is also located "far above all rule and authority and power and dominion, and above every name that is named, not only in this age but also in the one to come" (Eph 1:21).

The theme of Christ's exaltation to the right hand of God appears often in the New Testament, both in Paul and other New Testament writers.[2] However, the concept of the exalted messianic king, seated at the right hand of God, derives originally from Psalm 110:1: "The LORD says to my Lord: 'Sit at my right hand, until I make your enemies your footstool.'" The image, then, is one of enthronement, authority, and transcendent power, specifically as

2. See: Mark 16:19; Luke 22:69; Acts 2:37; 5:31; 7:55, 56; Rom 8:34; 2 Cor 6:7; Col 3:1; Heb 1:3; 10:12; 12:12; 1 Pet 3:22.

it relates to the aforementioned "enemies." By describing Christ in this language, Paul acknowledges the realities of the evil spiritual powers that stand in opposition to Christ, while still unflinchingly affirming the absolute supremacy of the power of Christ above and over "all rule and authority and power and dominion"[3] that would contest him (Eph 1:21). Thus, the exalted Christ is more than just one of many spiritual beings in the heavenly realm. He is the sovereign Lord and ruler of all. He is *Christus Victor* and the divine warrior, who triumphs over all rival powers.

Paul then makes another brief Old Testament allusion as he states: "And he put all things under his feet and gave him as head over all things to the church" (Eph 1:22). The phrase "all things under his feet" comes directly from Psalm 8:6: "You have given him dominion over the works of your hands; you have put all things under his feet."[4] With this statement, Paul attributes to Christ the restored dominion that God apportioned to mankind in the garden of Eden but was then compromised due to Adam's rebellion and sin (cf. Gen 1:28; 3:15). As Anglican theologian John Stott notes: " . . . the full dominion which God intended man to enjoy is now exercised only by the man Christ Jesus."[5] Thus, as the God-man, Christ's resurrection and ascension effect a reclamation of the authority that was intended for humanity at creation but was later abdicated to Satan and his forces at the fall.

However, the Pauline proclamations concerning the power of God are not abstract theological assertions alone. Earlier in Ephesians 1, Paul emphasizes that this tremendous power directly benefits God's people who are "in Christ" (Eph 1:3–14). His statements about the power of God in Ephesians 1:19–21 are situated in the thanksgiving and prayer of verses 1:15–23. Stott rightly describes this section as a blessing directed toward God "for having blessed

3. Darko suggests these four terms compose a "representative list encapsulating the totality of these powers." Darko, *Against Powers and Principalities*, 90.

4. The wording in Ephesians 1:22 is nearly identical with the LXX translation of the same phrase in Psalm 8:6.

5. Stott, *God's New Society*, 60.

us in Christ" and prayer to the effect "that God [would] open our eyes to grasp the fullness of this blessing."[6] Paul, thus, desires his readers not only to know about this blessing; he wants them to experience and actively *participate* in this blessing as well. The "immeasurable greatness of his power" in Ephesians 1:21, thus, equates to the Christ-resurrecting, enemy-defeating, dominion-reclaiming power of God "toward us who believe."

That Paul desires believers to appreciate and appropriate this power is further echoed in the prayer of Ephesians 3:14–21, in which Paul pleads "that according to the riches of his glory he may grant you to be strengthened with power through his Spirit in your inner being, so that Christ may dwell in your hearts through faith . . ." (3:16–17a). This "power" (*dynamei*) is the same as the "power" (*dynameōs*) of 1:19. However, the Ephesians 3 text shows that this power is also a fully Trinitarian power in that it is from God the Father (3:14–15), given through the Holy Spirit (Eph 3:16) so that Christ might dwell in the hearts of Christian believers (3:17). The Holy Spirit strengthens the believer with this power within his or her "inner being"; that is, the most profound and enduring part of a person (cf. 2 Cor 4:6). This power is inexhaustible and infinite, as God is "able to do far more abundantly than all that we ask or think, according to the power (*dynamin*) at work within us" (3:20).

As Ephesians is one of the "Prison Letters," it is possible that Paul borrows the image of the armor of God from the Roman soldiers who kept watch over his imprisonment. However, as mentioned in the chapter 7, it is clear that Paul has Isaiah 59:17 in view when writing this passage. Recall that in Isaiah 59, the dominant image is of God defending his people, when they are too weak to defend themselves. Thus, when a Christian experientially appropriates what is indicatively true of all believers in Christ, he or she is able to "be strong in the Lord and in the strength of his might" (Eph 6:10). Notably, Ephesians 6:10–20 does not teach Christian individuals to equip individual sets of spiritual armor. Rather, the "armor" of Ephesians 6 is a singular entity. It is the armor, not of

---

6. Stott, *God's New Society*, 51–52.

believers, but, "of God." Yahweh himself goes forth as the divine warrior to fight and gain victory on behalf of his people.[7]

Likewise, Paul teaches Christians to fight evil forces not in their own strength, but rather to "stand" (*stēnai*)[8] in Christ. Christ is the warrior. Christ is the victor. He is the one who is supreme over all supernatural beings. For Paul, then, spiritual warfare cannot be a man-centered endeavor, but rather a thoroughly Christ-centered reality. Thus, Paul structures Ephesians around a conceptual *inclusio* referring to the church's position, power, and blessings in Christ. Thus, to equip the armor of God (Eph 6:10–20) is simply to accept and appropriate all that is true of one who is in Christ (Eph 1:3–14) so as "to stand against the schemes of the devil . . . against the rulers, against the authorities, against the cosmic powers over this present darkness, against the spiritual forces of evil in the heavenly places" (Eph 6:11–12).

It is over these powers that Christ has won a decisive spiritual victory, and as a result, the Ephesian Christians are no longer under the dominion of dark spiritual forces. Rather, as Christ has been raised from the dead by the power of God (Eph 1:19), they too have been made "alive together in Christ" (Eph 2:5). Instead of belonging to the "world" or the present "age," they are now seated "in the heavenly places in Christ," who is enthroned at the right hand of God (Eph 2:6; 1:20). Thus, in saving the Ephesian Christians, Christ has effectively taken away what once belonged to the powers of evil. The Ephesian believers are, in effect, the spoils of spiritual war.

THE SPOILS OF SPIRITUAL WAR

The theme of spoils of spiritual war features prominently in Ephesians 4. In fact, while the word "power" (*dynamis*) is not explicitly used in Ephesians 4:1–16, there is a clear thematic connection between the power of Christ overcoming the powers of spiritual evil

---

7. See the discussion on Isaiah 59 in the chapter 7.

8. The root "*istēmi*" is used four times in the Ephesians 6:10–20 pericope.

and Paul's use of Psalm 68:18 in Ephesians 4:8: "Therefore it says, 'When he ascended on high he led a host of captives, and he gave gifts to men.'" Here Paul, yet again, connects Christ to Yahweh as the divine warrior king. Many have observed Paul's altering of the "receiving" of gifts in Psalm 68:18 to the "giving" of gifts in Ephesians 4:8. However, Paul's changing of "receiving" to "giving" in his quotation of Psalm 68:18 is not a mistake or haphazard usage of the Old Testament. Rather, Paul's change of "receiving" to "giving" is a necessary interpretive deduction from Psalm 68.[9] For in his victory, not only does Yahweh/Christ receive gifts, he also gives those same gifts to his people.

While some identify the "captives" of Ephesians 4:8 as the vanquished demonic forces themselves,[10] in light of the aforementioned observations, might it not be appropriate to connect the "captives" to the very "gifts" that are received by Christ and then given back to his church? Is it not possible that the captives are former gentile pagans, who were once under the dominion of the powers that ruled the nations, but are now saved by Christ; taken as spoil from those powers, and then given to the church as apostles, prophets, evangelists, and pastor-teachers (Eph 4:11)?

To put it more concretely, once places like the shores of Northern Africa, the Alpine mountains of Europe, and the island of Great Britain were under the spiritual dominion of demonic powers (cf. Deut 32:8). People born in such places were "dead in [their] trespasses and sins" and "strangers to the covenants of promise, having no hope and without God in the world" (Eph 2:1, 12). But God, through Christ's life, death, resurrection, and ascension, has delegitimized the authority that such powers possessed over gentile peoples and lands so that they might become "the LORD's portion" (Deut 32:9). Thus, from these once pagan people groups and lands, God will claim for himself people like Augustine, Calvin, and Julian of Norwich so as to give these redeemed gentiles to the church for the building up of Christ's body (Eph 4:8, 11).

9. See the previous discussion of Psalm 68 in chapter 7.

10. Arnold, *Magic and Power*, 56.

10

The Mystery of the Gospel

MYSTERY UNVEILED

The long-awaited messiah of the Jewish people has revealed himself to be the savior of people from all nations. While predicted and prefigured in Old Testament scripture, the inclusion of the gentiles into God's covenant people seems to fill Paul with rhapsodic wonder and profound astonishment. More than merely included, the "Gentiles are fellow heirs, members of the same body, and partakers of the promise in Christ Jesus through the gospel" (Eph 3:6). Once a murderous zealot and cultural chauvinist, Paul now recognizes that, in Christ, God has "broken down . . . the dividing wall of hostility" that stood between the people of the nations and the people of God (Eph 2:14). The gentile inclusion was not a divine afterthought or last-minute adjustment, but rather a part of "the plan of the mystery hidden for ages in God, who created all things" (Eph 3:9).

The term "mystery" (*mystērion*) becomes one of Paul's favorite terms when describing the good news for the gentiles (Rom 11:25; Eph 3:3, 4, 6, 9; Col 1:26 –27, 1 Tim 3:16). Mystery (*mystērion*) means "the unmanifested or private counsel of God . . . the secret thoughts, plans, and dispensations of God . . . which are hidden [from] human reason, as well as [from] all other comprehension below the divine level, and await either fulfillment or revelation to those for whom they are intended."[1] Once the mystery of the gentiles' place in the plan of God was hidden from the eyes of "the sons of men of other generations" (Eph 3:5), as well as the "rulers (*archais*) and authorities (*exousias*) in the heavenly places" (3:10) that held the nations in spiritual bondage. But now this mystery has been gloriously unveiled in Christ!

Paul has been divinely granted "stewardship" of ministering the mystery of this gospel to the gentiles (3:7). Moreover, with this assignment has come a corresponding authority, "by the working of his power (*dynameōs*)" (3:7). Herein lies another aspect of Paul's theology of power. The same "power" that rose Jesus from the dead (1:19) and subdues all spiritual "power[s]" (*dynameōs*) of darkness (1:21) is the same "power" (*dynameōs*) that fuels Paul's ministry of the gospel of grace.[2] Paul requires such power from outside of himself, for in proclaiming the gospel to the gentiles, he is engaging in nothing less than spiritual warfare with the powers who have held dominion over the nations (cf. 6:10–20).

A NEW WAY OF LIFE

In Romans, the "power (*dynamis*) of God" in the gospel is "for salvation to everyone who believes, to the Jew first and also to the Greek" (Rom 1:16). The power of God is at work not only to bring about the gentiles' faith, but also their "obedience" (Rom 15:18–19). So too, in Colossians, Paul will pray without ceasing that the gentile Christians of Colossae will "walk in a manner worthy of the Lord . . . being strengthened with all power (*dynamei*)" (Col 1:10–11), for they have been "delivered . . . from the domain of darkness" and "transferred . . . to the kingdom of his beloved Son" (Col 1:13).

Herein lies an important qualification: while it is true that Christ possesses supreme dominion over the powers of darkness,

---

1. BDAG 662.

2. Foulkes, *Ephesians*, 102.

this does not mean that those powers have altogether vanished from the world. Christians share in and have access to the victory of Christ over the powers, but they are by no means immune to the influence of the powers.[3] Thus, gentile believers must actively cast-off allegiance to and the way of life associated with the spiritual forces that once enslaved the pagan nations to sin (Eph 4:17–32; cf. Gal 4:8–9, 5:1). Gentile Christians "must no longer walk as the Gentiles do" (Eph 4:17).

Thus, the moral discourse in Ephesians may even be subtly connected to the rejection of specific deities associated with first century A.D. pagan culture in Asia Minor. For example, the exhortation, "And do not get drunk with wine, for that is debauchery, but be filled with the Spirit" (Eph 5:18) may be targeted against ritualistic worship of Dionysius.[4] Moreover, the command "In all circumstances take up the shield of faith, with which you can extinguish all the flaming darts of the evil one" (Eph 6:16) may reference Artemis, the patron goddess of Ephesus, whose primary weapon was a bow and arrow.[5]

In a similar vein, the *Haustefeln* (or "household codes") of the New Testament (Eph 5:21—6:9; Col 3:18—4:1; 1 Pt 2:13—3:7) can also be viewed in light of Christ's victory over the powers, wherein fellow Christians are commanded to relate with one another in participation with and anticipation of God's New Creation.[6] As New Testament scholar Benjamin Gladd writes: "Christ's work on the cross and his resurrection not only deliver individuals from their spiritual plight; they also restore a host of fractured relationships—cosmic, ethnic, familial, and so on."[7]

Simply said, communal identity is derivative of spiritual authority; spiritual authority is determinative for one's moral

3. Darko, *Against Powers and Principalities*, 112.

4. Darko, *Against Powers and Principalities*, 38–40, 136–137.

5. Darko, *Against Powers and Principalities*, 155.

6. Gladd, "Philemon." In *A Biblical-Theological Introduction to the New Testament* 404–405.

7. Gladd, "Philemon." In *A Biblical-Theological Introduction to the New Testament* 401.

behavior. When a person becomes a Christian, he or she is transferred from being under the authority of the spiritual powers, as well as the communal identity and moral behavior associated with the dominion of the powers. So, while a Christian retains his or her national or ethnic identity, that identity must no longer determine one's ultimate allegiance, values, or standard of behavior. For this reason, Paul declares, "Here there is not Greek and Jew, circumcised and uncircumcised, barbarian, Scythian, slave, free; but Christ is all, and in all" (Col 3:11; cf. Gal 3:28). Believers have been given a new community and a new way of life flowing from a new identity that supersedes any national identity or loyalty. No wonder Paul can count the impressive accolades of his Jewish national identity as "rubbish" when compared to "the surpassing worth" of knowing Jesus as Lord (Phil 3:7–8), and no wonder he can extol the "citizenship in heaven" above the privilege of Roman citizenship to the Christians of Philippi (Phil 3:20).[8]

Therefore, division on the basis of national identity has no place in the body of Christ. Through the redemptive accomplishment of Jesus, believing Jews and gentiles are reconciled to God and one another: "For he himself is our peace, who has made us both one and has broken down in his flesh the dividing wall of hostility . . . that he might create in himself one new man in place of the two, so making peace" (Eph 2:14–15). Yet, while Christ creates this trans-national unity, it is the task of the church to actively maintain this unity:[9]

> I therefore, a prisoner for the Lord, urge you to walk in
> a manner worthy of the calling to which you have been
> called, with all humility and gentleness, with patience,
> bearing with one another in love, eager to maintain the

8. " . . . under the provisions of the Roman form of constitutional government conferred on the city by Octavian in 42 B.C., Philippi was 'governed as if it was on Italian soil and its administration reflected that of Rome in almost every respect'. So, writing to Christians in a city proud of its relation to Rome, Paul tells the Philippians that they belong to a heavenly commonwealth, that is, their state and constitutive government is in heaven, and as its citizens they are to reflect its life." O'Brien, *The Epistle to the Philippians*, 461.

9. Darko, *Against Powers and Principalities*, 118.

unity of the Spirit in the bond of peace. There is one body and one Spirit—just as you were called to the one hope that belongs to your call—one Lord, one faith, one baptism, one God and Father of all, who is over all and through all and in all (Eph 4:1–6).

For this reason, at Antioch, Paul will rebuke Peter for sharing table fellowship with Christian Jews, but not Christian gentiles (Gal 2:11–21). Such conduct is "not in step with the truth of the gospel" (Gal 2:14). Division in the body of Christ is a shame to the church and a poor witness to unbelievers (cf. 1 Cor 6:1–8). But when Christians are one in Christ—Jew and gentile, black and white, African and Asian—it is a display of "the manifold wisdom of God," not only to the watching world, but also to "the rulers and authorities in the heavenly places," over whom Christ has triumphed (Eph 3:10).

11

Artemis of the Ephesians is Deposed

A CASE STUDY

While the preceding analysis shows Paul's theology of the powers, Luke's account of Paul's time in the city of Ephesus may provide a glimpse of what this theology looks like in ministerial practice. When Paul arrives in the great city of Ephesus, he spends his first three months boldly preaching about the kingdom of God in a Jewish synagogue (Acts 19:8) until some of the local Jews rise up and expel him and his disciples (19:9).[1] Paul then takes this group of new converts, composed of both Jews and gentiles, and they essentially become the founding core of the Ephesian church. They relocate to the "Hall of Tyrannus," where Paul teaches daily for two full years and has a profoundly influential ministry that shatters nationalistic enclaves (19:9–10). During this time, " . . . all

---

1. "Paul's association with the synagogue lasted for three months, which was longer than usual. It was brought to an end by the opposition of some of the Jews who were hardened against the message, refused to believe it, and spoke against it (cf. 13:45; 18:6). The strength of the opposition was such that Paul felt that he could no longer use the synagogue as a base for evangelism, and he therefore moved to neutral ground, just as he had done in Corinth." Marshall, *Acts*, 327.

the residents of Asia [i.e., Asia Minor] heard the word of the Lord, both Jews and Greeks" (19:10). Thus, it is likely during this period that the church of Colossae and the seven churches mentioned in Revelation 2—3, among several others, were planted. As Kent Hughes observes, "By any estimate, what happened in those two years is amazing."[2]

Likewise, Acts 19 emphasizes the supernatural nature of Paul's ministry during his time in Ephesus. The Holy Spirit works through Paul, powerfully validating the Apostle's ministry of the gospel with displays of healing and the casting out of demons (19:11). Apparently, this was happening so often that people attempted to take "handkerchiefs or aprons" that Paul had touched so that they could bring them to sick or demonized people for healing (19:12a).

The "seven sons" of a supposed high priest named Sceva also take note of Paul's ministry (Acts 19:14). Whether or not he was actually descended from priestly ancestry can neither proven or falsified. As New Testament scholar I. Howard Marshall notes: "Either Sceva was simply a member of a high-priestly family, or he assumed the title for professional purposes in order to impress and delude the public, since a high priest (or his sons) would have close contact with the supernatural; we may compare the way in which modern quacks take such titles as 'Doctor' or 'Professor.'"[3]

These Jewish exorcists claim to have power over demonic forces (19:13a). They see how influential Paul's ministry is so they decide to add another spell to their repertoire: " . . . I adjure you by the Jesus whom Paul proclaims" (19:13b). However, when they encounter a demonized man, the demon acknowledges its awareness of both Jesus and Paul, but also that it has never heard of the sons of Sceva (19:15). Following this exchange, the demonized man proceeds to leap on the sons of Sceva, "master[ing]" and "overpower[ing]" them all, after which these men flee naked and wounded from the house in which they were ministering (19:16). This event apparently makes a significant impact in the city of

2. Hughes, *Acts*, 255.

3. Marshall, *Acts*, 329.

Ephesus. Not only are the Ephesians confronted with the reality of evil spiritual forces, but they recognize the categorically unique spiritual power associated with Jesus: "And fear fell upon them all, and the name of the Lord Jesus was extolled" (19:17).

Even Ephesian "believers" who had not yet repented of practicing "magic arts" become convicted of their sin and renounce these pagan habits, even burning costly, hand-written books (19:18–20; cf. Eph 4:17). As Clinton E. Arnold comments concerning these "magical arts": "Magic [in western Asia Minor] was primarily concerned with the acquisition of supernatural powers and the manipulation of the spirit world in the interest of the magician."[4] Thus, this act of corporate repentance would have deeply impacted the city of Ephesus, which had a reputation of magical practices as a regular part of daily life.[5] The end result of the Ephesian Christians' rejection of magic was further evangelization: "So the word of the Lord continued to increase mightily" (19:20). In fact, the word of the Lord increases so mightily that the even socio-economic climate of the city of Ephesus undergoes adjustment, as the idol-making business surrounding the worship of Artemis begins to crash.[6]

To underscore the extraordinary nature of this transformation, Ephesus was the international center for the cult of the earth-mother goddess Artemis. Ephesus housed the famed temple of Artemis, one of the seven wonders of the ancient world. The worship of Artemis functioned as nothing less than one of the vital cultural and economic pillars of life in Ephesus. As Arnold notes of

4. Arnold, *Magic and Power*, 20.

5. Kidd suggests that Arnold's contextual analysis may even shed light on the cultural situation surrounding the Colossian heresy, as the cultural situation of Ephesus (as the leading city of Asia Minor) may have influenced Colossae. Kidd, "Ephesians: Power and Magic: The Concept of Power in Ephesians in Light of Its Historical Setting," 203.

6. Darko notes that the inhabitants of Ephesus seemed to have "established a connection between the powers of Artemis and the Ephesian Grammata [an Ephesian magical formula/spell]." Thus, the rejection of magical books may have also entailed an implicit rejection of the worship of Artemis. Darko, *Against Powers and Principalities*, 36.

Artemis Ephesia, "unsurpassed cosmic power [was] attributed to her."[7] But this situation changes when the Christian gospel breaks into the city. Paul has persuaded many Ephesians that " . . . gods made with hands are not gods" (19:26).

Here, it is important to remember Paul's somewhat complex understanding of idols. In 1 Corinthians Paul bluntly states that "an idol has no real existence," for "there is no God but one" (1 Cor 4:8). Yet, in the same breath he acknowledges, "For although there may be so-called gods in heaven or on earth—as indeed there are many "gods" and many "lords"— yet for us there is one God, the Father, from whom are all things and for whom we exist, and one Lord, Jesus Christ, through whom are all things and through whom we exist" (1 Cor 8:5–6). So, while idols do not possess the attributes of God's divinity, that is not to say that idols lack association with real spiritual (i.e., demonic) entities. A little later in the same letter, he makes the argument in even clearer terms: "What do I imply then? That food offered to idols is anything, or that an idol is anything? No, I imply that what pagans sacrifice they offer to demons and not to God. I do not want you to be participants with demons. You cannot drink the cup of the Lord and the cup of demons. You cannot partake of the table of the Lord and the table of demons" (1 Cor 10:19–21). Thus, there should be little doubt that Paul would have understood the worship of Artemis as participation in and with a demonic power who historically held vast influence over Ephesus and the region of Asia Minor.

Eventually, a silversmith named Demetrius gathers other people in his industry, and together, they incite a riot in fearful protest of Paul's ministry (Acts 19: 24–34). Demetrius's words are telling: "And there is danger not only that this trade of ours may come into disrepute but also that the temple of the great goddess Artemis may be counted as nothing, and that she may even be deposed from her magnificence, she whom all Asia and the world worship" (19:27). In essence, Demetrius notices that the Ephesian economy is suffering, and offers a religious solution to restore the former glory of Ephesus. In a move reminiscent of nationalist

---

7. Arnold, *Magic and Power*, 21.

fervor, Demetrius seeks to spark a populist revival of the worship of Artemis, the patron goddess of Ephesus. Yet, despite the ensuing frenzied shouts of "Great is Artemis of the Ephesians!" and fierce opposition, Paul and the Ephesian Christians are nevertheless able to continue declaring and displaying the reign of the Lord Jesus Christ (19:35–41). One might even say, the great goddess Artemis had been placed underneath the feet of Christ (cf. Eph 1:22).[8]

Moreover, in light of Acts 19, Paul's contrast of the power of God and the powers of evil in his letter to the Ephesians cannot be understood as mere generic or speculative theologizing. Instead, Paul is pastorally addressing a deeply specific and contextual issue for the Ephesian church, and, likely, much of western Asia Minor. The epistle to the Ephesians reminds Paul's original readers that, over against the power of Artemis and all other spiritual forces, Christ alone is supreme and sufficient.

SUMMARY OF PART III

Paul understands himself as an apostle sent to preach the gospel of Jesus Christ to the gentile nations. In line with the "Deuteronomy 32 worldview," he views gentiles, who are outside of Christ, as being under the spiritual authority of the powers of darkness. Through the "elemental spirits of the world" (*stoichea*), the powers enslave the nations to cultural norms and idolatrous ethnic/national allegiances that are akin to what contemporary readers would identify as various forms of nationalism. The powers strive to seduce even the people of God to relapse into such loyalties, and, as a result, live in a way that contrary to life in Christ.

---

8. "It is very interesting that Luke associates such prolific demonic activity with Ephesus . . . . Luke does not describe any other location with so many accounts of the demonic in Acts . . . . The evidence does make us wonder why Luke would choose Ephesus to illustrate how the gospel of Jesus Christ has the power to overcome the demonic realm. If Ephesus and its environs were reputed as a center for 'demonic' activity, Luke's purpose of demonstrating the superior power of the gospel would be well established by this account." Arnold, *Magic and Power*, 30.

However, while such powers possess true authority and influence, the power of Christ is infinitely greater. By his death, resurrection, and ascension, Christ delegitimized the dominion of the powers over the nations. The contrast between the power of God and the powers of darkness is a major theme of the Pauline letters, especially his letter to the Ephesians. Having been delivered from the kingdom of darkness, gentile believers are to reflect their submission and allegiance to Christ through their new communal identity in the church and their moral behavior, which must no longer accord with their former gentile way of life.

A vivid picture of Paul's theology of powers is presented in Acts 19, in which Luke recounts Paul's ministry in the city of Ephesus. The newly planted Ephesian church flourishes as a multi-cultural church that testifies to the gospel's power that breaks down nationalistic barriers that once stood between Jews and gentiles in Ephesus. Moreover, as the gospel continues to influence the lives of Ephesian Christians, Artemis (the patron goddess of the city) is deposed from her position of former authority and glory.

Part IV

CHRISTIANITY
AND NATIONALISM

12

DEMONS HAVE DOCTRINES

A SYSTEMATIC THEOLOGY OF NATIONALISM

In his first letter to Timothy, Paul writes, "Now the Spirit expressly says that in later times some will depart from the faith by devoting themselves to deceitful spirits and teachings of demons" (1 Tim 4:1). Here, the Apostle announces that false teachers will arise within the believing community, depart from sound doctrine, and attempt to lead God's people into heresy and apostasy. The source of the heretical message of the false teachers lies in "deceitful spirits," who actively promote "teachings of demons."[1] In a similar vein of thought, Paul elsewhere describes the false apostles who seek to infiltrate the church as "ministers of Satan" (2 Cor 11:15). Simply said, demons have doctrines.

If nationalism possesses a demonic aspect, as the biblical analysis of the previous chapters have shown, then it should not surprise us that nationalism (in its various forms) would also come with a constellation of beliefs that both mirror and oppose the Christian gospel. Thus, the subsequent chapters of this section will introduce and briefly explore what one might call a systematic theology of nationalism.

---

1. Towner, *The Letters to Timothy and Titus*, 290.

By way of approach, I will adopt a similar methodology as J. Gresham Machen, who a century ago sought to clearly differentiate the doctrines of theological liberalism from that of historic Christianity in his book *Christianity and Liberalism*.[2] Yet, while Machen engaged the beliefs of liberalism which he found to be most at odds with Christianity, the next few chapters will utilize the various core doctrines of Christianity, as found in the Apostles' Creed, to frame how nationalism has sought to subvert and supplant those Christian doctrines with its own parodistic beliefs. In full, the Apostles' Creed reads:

> I believe in God the Father, Almighty, Maker of heaven and earth;
> And in Jesus Christ, his only begotten Son, our Lord;
> Who was conceived by the Holy Ghost, born of the Virgin Mary
> Suffered under Pontius Pilate; was crucified, dead and buried;
> He descended into hell.
> The third day he rose again from the dead;
> He ascended into heaven, and sits at the right hand of God the Father Almighty,
> From thence he shall come to judge the quick and the dead
> I believe in the Holy Ghost;
> I believe a holy catholic church; the communion of saints,
> The forgiveness of sins,
> The resurrection of the body,
> And the life everlasting. Amen.[3]

Many examples of nationalism in the following discussion will reflect my own historical familiarity and experience within the American variety of nationalism. However, as chapter 3 showed, nationalism is a variegated phenomenon that is not bound to any one nation, ethnicity, political ideology, or even historical era. Thus, I will also seek to show historical instances of nationalist doctrine—both ancient and modern—from around the globe.

---

2. Machen, *Christianity and Liberalism*.

3. *Historic Creeds and Confessions*.

I BELIEVE IN GOD THE FATHER, ALMIGHTY

The Decalogue begins with the doctrine of God: "And God spoke all these words, saying, 'I am the LORD your God, who brought you out of the land of Egypt, out of the house of slavery. You shall have no other gods before me'" (Exod 20:1–3). The first commandment demands not only belief in the existence of God, but that God is to be worshipped above all. Commenting on the first commandment, Luther teaches in his *Small Catechism*, "We must fear, love, and trust God *more than anything else*" (emphasis added).[4] Positively, the first commandment requires a Christian to see God as his or her highest good to whom highest allegiance is due. Negatively, a Christian is "to avoid placing anything other than the true God ahead of him in our thoughts, actions, and affections."[5] Nationalism, then, necessarily stands against the demands of the first commandment and the Christian understanding of God as the one to whom highest praise and devotion belongs. Afterall, part of the "core doctrine of nationalism" is the belief that "loyalty to the nation overrides all other loyalties."[6]

Through such fervent loyalty of its adherents, the god of nationalism is able to acquire great power and glory. For this reason, despite Roman society's cultural and civic observance of the Olympian religion, Augustine of Hippo observes that a nationalist devotion to the glory of Rome, not Jove, was the true god of the Roman people: " . . . the Roman empire was not extended and preserved by the worship of these gods [the Olympians] . . . . Glory they [the Romans] most ardently loved: for it they wished to live,

---

4. Luther, *Small Catechism*, 5.

5. Frame, *The Doctrine of the Christian Life*, 407.

6. Anthony D. Smith describes the "core doctrine" of nationalism as the following six propositions: "1.) the world is divided into nations, each with its own character, history, and destiny; 2.) the nation is the sole source of political power, 3.) loyalty to the nation overrides all other loyalties; 4.) to be free, every individual must belong to a nation; 5.) every nation requires full self-expression and autonomy; 6.) global peace and justice require a world of autonomous nations." Smith, *Nationalism*, 25.

for it they did not hesitate to die. Every other desire was repressed by the strength of their passion for that one thing."[7]

In exhorting his fellow members of the Brazilian military toward a similar vision of singular, nationalist commitment, General Golbery do Cuoto e Silva writes:

> To be a nationalist is to be always ready to give up any doctrine, any theory, any ideology, feelings, passions, ideals, and values, as soon as they appear to be incompatible with the supreme loyalty which is due to the Nation above everything else. Nationalism is, must be, and cannot possibly be other than an Absolute One in itself, and its purpose is as well an Absolute End—at least as long as the Nation continues as such. There is no place, nor should there be, nor could there be place for nationalism as a simple instrument to another purpose that transcends it.[8]

In a nationalist framework, then, worshipping Jesus is not necessarily an issue of concern, so long as devotion to Jesus does not override supreme loyalty to the nation. The god(s) of nationalism will accommodate Christians who comply with the command to make sacrifices to the Roman emperor[9] or replace crosses in their churches with posters of Chinese President Xi Jinping.[10] Nationalism welcomes syncretism, but anathematizes those who would claim absolute allegiance to the one who has been given all authority in heaven and on earth (Matt 28:18).

In addition to casting the nation as the object of highest worship and devotion, nationalism mimics the Christian doctrine of God by attributing parental qualities to the nation, particularly the land of the nation. Many nations refer to their territory as the "fatherland" or "motherland," because, as Grosby notes, "the

---

7. Augustine of Hippo, "The City of God," bk. 5, ch.12.

8. Cuoto e Silva, *Geopolítica do Brasil*, 101.

9. Pate, "Revelation 2–19 and the Roman Imperial Cult," 69.

10. Kate Shellnutt, "China Tells Christians to Replace Images of Jesus with Communist President," https://www.christianitytoday.com/news/2017/november/china-christians-jesus-communist-president-xi-jinping-yugan.html

parental power to generate and transmit life is dependent upon the sustenance that is provided by the land in the form of fruits, produce and so on. Implicit in this attribution is the recognition that the land itself is a source of life." [11] Even the etymology behind the word "nation," derived from the Latin *natio/nasci*, "to be born from," casts the god of nationalism in a parental light. [12]

In its doctrine of God, nationalism also tends to personify the nation into a mythical being. As the god Ashur was seen as the spiritual embodiment of the Assyrian empire (see discussion in chapter 6), so too modern nations take on the personalities of quasi-deities, such as Uncle Sam of the United States, John Bull of England, or Marianne of France. [13] While the personality of Uncle Sam did not manifest until the War of 1812, since the time before the American Revolution, American nationalists have character-ized Columbia (or Freedom) as the patron goddess of the United States, whose graven image is enshrined in the Statue of Liberty and whose name adorns the nation's capital city (i.e., the District *of Columbia*). [14]

In the modern era, the flags have similarly tended to function beyond a mere identifying symbol of a nation, and, instead, have been imbued with sacred significance and accorded ritualistic worship. As historian Carlton J.H. Hayes notes: "There are univer-sal liturgical forms for 'saluting' the flag, for 'dipping' the flag, for 'lowering' the flag, and for 'hoisting' the flag. Men bare their heads when the flag passes by; and in praise of the flag poets write odes, and to it children sing hymns and pledge allegiance." [15] In this way, the flag functions as an icon for the deity of nationalism. Thus, when Vice President Mike Pence exhorts his fellow Americans to " . . . run the race marked out for us. Let's fix our eyes on Old Glory

11. Grosby, *Nationalism*, 45.

12. Grosby, *Nationalism*, 44.

13. Hayes, *Nationalism*, 164.

14. A graven image of Columbia also adorns the top of the U.S. Capitol Building. John Higham "Indian Princess and Roman Goddess: The First Fe-male Symbols of America," 63.

15. Hayes, *Nationalism*, 167.

and all she represents . . . "[16], his words appeal to an inherently religious impulse. By quoting Hebrews 12:2, but substituting "Jesus" with "Old Glory," who is personified as a female deity, Pence places the American flag "and all *she* represents" as the object of spiritual focus and devotion. Although spoken by a professed Christian, such words do not reflect the religion of Christianity, but that of nationalism.

MAKER OF HEAVEN AND EARTH

The doctrine of creation is often considered a part of the doctrine of God in Christian dogmatics. This crucial article of faith "stresses the fact that God is the origin of all things, and that all things belong to Him and are subject to Him."[17] However, the doctrine of creation also serves a pivotal point in the meta-narrative through Christians understand their identity as the people. In other words, Genesis not only records the beginnings of the cosmos and the nations of the world, it recounts the beginnings of Abraham and the family of God's people. In a similar way, the Babylonian creation account of the *Enuma Elish* not only furnishes an account of how mankind and the universe was made, it tells the story of the origins of the Babylonian people and their patron deity Marduk.[18] Thus, the *Enuma Elish* is not only a creation account; it is a creation account with a nationalist aim.

While not all varieties of nationalism have a unique account of the origin of the cosmos, the theme of "sacred foundations of nations" has played a significant role in how nations have cultivated a sense of national identity.[19] Anthony D. Smith has observed that the notion of sacred foundations of nationalism furnish:

---

16. Pence, "Transcript: Mike Pence's RNC Speech," https://www.cnn.com/2020/08/26/politics/mike-pence-speech-transcript/index.html

17. Berkhof, *Systematic Theology*, 126.

18. "The Creation Epic." In *ANET* 60–72.

19. Smith, *Nationalism*, 153.

1. a belief in ethnic election, the idea of the nation as a chosen people, entrusted with a special mission or having an exclusive covenant with the deity;

2. an attachment to a sacred territory, an ancestral homeland sanctified by the saints, heroes and sages, as well as the tombs and monuments of the ancestors;

3. shared memories of the "golden ages," as the high points of the nation's ethno-history, ages of material and/or spiritual and artistic splendor;

4. the cult of the "glorious dead," and their heroic self-sacrifice on behalf of the nation and its destiny.[20]

Some of the most successful political leaders in history have recognized the powers of national creation accounts and have even gone to great lengths to synthesize such mythologies for their nations. For example, Caesar Augustus intentionally commissioned Virgil to write the *Aeneid*, which recounts the story of Aeneas and a remnant of Trojan warriors, who escape the ruins of Asiatic Troy for the promised land of the Italian peninsula. Here, by the will of Jove, Aeneas will become the Abraham-like patriarch, whose sacred task it will be to "found the Roman people."[21]

So too, even in the modern era, the sacred foundations of nations have not disappeared. Indeed, "the 'political religion' of secular nationalism continues to draw on older religious motifs for its liturgy, symbolism, and myth-making."[22] For instance, well into the twentieth century, President Lyndon B. Johnson writes: "They came here—the exile and the stranger, brave but frightened—to find a place where a man could be his own man. They made a covenant with this land . . . and it binds us still. If we keep its terms, we shall flourish."[23]

20. Smith, *Nationalism*, 155.

21. Virgil, *The Aeneid*, bk. 1, lines 46–49.

22. Smith, *Nationalism*, 154.

23. Johnson, "Inaugural Address of Lyndon B. Johnson," https://avalon.law.yale.edu/20th_century/johnson.asp

Thus, while human societies have always shown a proclivity to exalt nations to a place of spiritual ultimacy, nationalism (in its contemporary forms) seems to offer a theology of God that uniquely befits the secular age. Over and against the Christian doctrine of God, nationalism provides a this-worldly god that fills the religious void left in the wake of naturalist materialism by offering "a substitute for, or supplement to, historic supernatural religion."[24] However, unlike the Christian God, who is transcendent, righteous, and contingent upon nothing, the god of nationalism is thoroughly immanentized, capable of horrific evil, and completely dependent upon the devotion of its adherents for power.

---

24. Hayes, *Nationalism*, 176

13

THE CHRISTOLOGY
OF NATIONALISM

JESUS CHRIST . . . CONCEIVED BY THE HOLY
SPIRIT, BORN OF THE VIRGIN MARY

Christians believe that salvation is only made possible by the God-
man, the Lord Jesus Christ. Only a man could endure the penalty
of sin, and only God could defeat its power. Only Christ who is
both completely God and completely man could accomplish the
miracle of redemption. However, nationalism tends to co-opt the
Christian doctrine of Christ by attributing human national leaders
with divine and messianic qualities.

In ancient Egypt, the Pharaoh was "of divine essence, a god
incarnate," who descended to reign among men.[1] In a similar
but slightly different characterization, Mesopotamian kings were
viewed as "great men" elevated to a position of divinity, whose task
lay in "maintaining harmonious relations between human society
and the supernatural powers."[2] Thus, in Egypt, the god descends
from heaven to earth, whereas in Mesopotamia, man ascends to

---

1. Frankfurt, *Kingship and the Gods*, 5
2. Frankfurt, *Kingship and the Gods*, 6.

heaven. Significantly, in both cases, the notion of kingship involves a type of dual nature.

Outside of the ancient Near East, Rome also sought to cast its leaders as possessing a measure of divine essence. For example, another fascinating purpose of *The Aeneid* lay in the ancient legend that Aeneas was supposedly the son of the goddess Venus. As members of the Julio-Claudio dynasty claimed to descend directly from Aeneas, *The Aeneid* functioned as a subtle reminder that Caesar Augustus was descended from a deity, and ruled with a divine mandate.

Even well into the modern era, the Japanese emperor was considered divine as well. In fact, the Meji Constitution of 1889 stated "The Emperor is sacred and inviable."[3] Only in 1946 did the Japanese emperor renounce a claim to divinity due to the conclusion of World War 2 and the Allied Occupation of Japan.

In the secular West, which is incredulous to any notion of the transcendent, attributing actual divinity to national leaders is not as common as it was in the pre-modern era. Nevertheless, nationalism continues to promote a type of Christology in the way it will often depict national leaders with messianic language and visual representations.

For Christians, Jesus is the seed of Abraham and the long-awaited heir of David. He is the anointed, messianic king who fulfills God's promises for his people. Similarly, nationalist ideology will often connect the rise of new political leaders with the providential plan of God. Thus, since the time of the Western Zhou Dynasty (c. 1045–771 B.C.), the Chinese nation has understood the legitimacy of its rulers on the basis of the "Mandate of Heaven"; an idea which continues to grant a divine sanction to the Chinese Communist Party into the present time.[4]

In contemporary American politics, Presidents can be portrayed in Christ-like iconography, regardless of party affiliation. In 2009, New York artist Michal D'Antuono painted *The Truth*

3. Kawai, "The Divinity of the Japanese Emperor," 3.

4. Zhao, "The Mandate of Heaven and Performance Legitimization in Historical and Contemporary China," 418, 428.

(President Obama) to celebrate the newly elected President's first hundred days in office. The painting seems to be critique of the American tendency to hoist messianic expectations upon political candidates but then (figuratively) crucify them when they inevitably fail to meet up to those expectations. The portrait depicts U.S. President Barack Obama in front of the Presidential seal, wearing a crown of thorns. In a direct *homage* to Matthias Grünewald's *Isenheim Altarpiece* (1512), the President's arms are raised in forty-five-degree angles, as if hanging from a cross. The image conveys a sense of the anointed one suffering unjustly, and perhaps even redemptively, at the hands of his political adversaries.

Michael D'Antuono, *The Truth (President Obama)*. 2009. Acrylic on canvas. www.artandresponse.com. Reproduced with permission from Michael D'Antuono.

In 2017, artist Jon McNaughton depicted President Donald Trump in a different yet equally messianic light in his piece *You Are Not Forgotten.*[5] In this painting, President Trump stands in front of the White House, surrounded by soldiers, veterans, members of law enforcement, and administration officials. A generic, blue-collar family waters a tender, young plant, " . . . like root out of dry ground" (Isa 53:2), as the President beneficently smiles. At

5. To view this copyrighted image, visit www.jonmcnaughton.com/patriotic/you-are-not-forgotten.

the base of the painting, a vanquished snake writhes, having been crushed underneath the foot of the American leader (cf. Gen 3:15; Rom 16:20). There is no irony, satire, or critique in McNaughton's presentation. Rather, it is a sincere depiction of Donald J. Trump as a type of Christ.

Ironically, while the Jewish people of the first century wanted their messiah to look like a political leader instead of Jesus, since the time of Christ, nationalism tends to envision political leaders *as Jesus*. While some leaders intentionally promote themselves as Christ-like anointed ones, and others have such depictions thrust upon them by zealous supporters, no fallible human leader is capable of bearing the weight of messianic expectations.

CRUCIFIED, DEAD, AND BURIED

At the cross, Jesus Christ accomplished the work of redemption. In his death, Christians find their life. By the "precious blood of Christ, like that of a lamb without blemish or spot," God's people have been "ransomed" (1 Pet 1:18–19). For this reason, Paul tells the Christians of Corinth, "For I decided to know nothing among you except Jesus Christ and him crucified" (1 Cor 2:2). This central and sacred doctrine of the Christian faith also finds a counterpart in the false gospel of nationalism.

Whereas the church is born of the blood of Christ, nations are born of the blood of soldiers and citizens, whose sacrifices are at times demanded by the gods of those nations. As Thomas Jefferson wrote, "What signify a few lives lost in a century or two? The tree of liberty must be refreshed from time to time with the blood of patriots and tyrants."[6] Through war comes peace; through death comes life; through violence comes redemption.

Those who give their lives in service to the nation are (tellingly) described as having made "the ultimate sacrifice."[7] War memo-

---

6. Jefferson, "From Thomas Jefferson to William Stephens Smith, 13 November 1787," https://founders.archives.gov/documents/Jefferson/01-12 -02-0348

7. I do not wish to diminish the service that soldiers have rendered their

rials and tombs to the "unknown soldier" are functional religious shrines.[8] In the United States, Memorial Day is a national holiday (literally a *holy* day) set aside to honor those who died for freedom (cf. Gal 5:1). All of these examples betray a temptation to accord spiritual, religious, and inherently Christological significance to the blood sacrifice of soldiers.

However, unlike the Christian doctrine of redemption in which God sacrifices himself for the salvation of his people, the nationalist doctrine of redemption is reversed. Through the blood of its people, the nation is saved. As British Prime Minister William Pitt once declared, in a statement that pithily describes the Pelagian nature of nationalist redemption, "England has saved herself by her exertions and will, as I trust, save Europe by her example."[9] Grace has no place in nationalism; for the nationalist, salvation comes by works and works alone.

HE ROSE FROM THE DEAD, HE ASCENDED TO HEAVEN . . . FROM THENCE HE SHALL COME TO JUDGE

The doctrine of the resurrection is the lynchpin of the Christian faith. Without the resurrection, Christianity has no gospel. Only if Christ has been truly raised from the dead can a Christian be united with him in that resurrection (Rom 6:5). As Paul says, "And if Christ has not been raised, your faith is futile and you are still in your sins. Then those also who have fallen asleep in Christ have perished. If in Christ we have hope in this life only, we are of all people most to be pitied" (1 Cor 15:17–19). Likewise, the

---

nations, especially those solders who lost their lives in defending their nations. However, the phrase "*ultimate* sacrifice," I believe, is a Christological phrase that should be rightly reserved solely for Christ's sacrifice on the cross.

8. Tombs of "the unknown soldier" are located in many modern nations. The more famous examples include the monuments located at Westminster Abbey in London, the Arc de Triomphe in Paris, Arlington Cemetery near Washington D.C., and the Ysukuni shrine in Tokyo. See: Grosby, *Nationalism*, 85–86.

9. Hastings, *The Construction of Nationhood*, 62–63.

Christian doctrines of ascension and the session at the right hand of God reflect the reality of Christ's reign over his people and victory over his enemies (Eph 1:19–21).[10] From heaven, Jesus Christ will return as the glorious and eternal Son of Man; the divine judge who stands at the end of history (Dan 7:13–14; Mark 14:62). Yet, here too, nationalism offers its own parody doctrines.

On January 1, 42 B.C., the Roman Senate declared Julius Caesar to be a god. This "apotheosis" came at the instigation of Octavian (later known as Augustus), as one means of consolidating his power over against his rival Mark Antony.[11] While novel at the time, deification of the Roman emperor, by senatorial vote, eventually became a standard practice after the emperor had died. Having died as men, emperors would be (figuratively) resurrected and worshipped as gods in the imperial cult. Under Domitian, emperor worship was made compulsory on threat of execution.[12]

Apotheosis of the emperors (and sometimes their family members) was often visually represented in coinage and sculpture by an eagle lifting the emperor's soul to the heavens in ascension.[13] More than a posthumous, political honor, the apotheosis of Roman emperors served a pragmatic purpose in engendering nationalist loyalty to the empire. L. Joseph Kreitzer observes, "The worship of the Roman emperor as the personification of divinity was used to great political advantage, particularly as a means of welding various peoples and cultures into a single empire."[14] Simply said, the deification of the Roman emperors united the empire by uniting the religious affections of the empire.

Fascinatingly, this impulse is not exclusively ancient. In 1865, the final year of the American Civil War, Greek-Italian artist Constantino Brumidi completed a fresco entitled *The Apotheosis of*

10. See the discussion on Christ's resurrection and ascension in chapter 9.

11. On another related note, by pushing through this vote, Octavian, who was the adopted son of Julius Caesar, effectively became the son of a god. See: Kreitzer, "Apotheosis of the Roman Emperor," 213.

12. Pate, "Revelation 2–19 and the Roman Imperial Cult," 69.

13. Kreitzer, "Apotheosis of the Roman Emperor," 211–212.

14. Kreitzer, "Apotheosis of the Roman Emperor," 216.

Washington, underneath the duomo of the United States Capitol Building.

Constantino Brumidi. *The Apotheosis of Washington.* 1865. Fresco. The United States Capitol Building, Washington D.C. Photograph courtesy of Mark Pellegrini.

Here, the founding father and first United States President, George Washington, sits enthroned like the Son of Man upon the clouds of heaven (cf. Dan 7:13–14). Beside him sit the goddesses Victoria (Victory) and Columbia (Freedom), and around the surrounding rim of the dome are a divine council of pagan gods and goddesses, including Neptune, Minerva, Mercury, Vulcan, and Ceres, each of whom serve a critical role in the developing the American nation's military and industrial might. Jupiter is conspicuously absent, as the deified President Washington sits upon the throne of heaven, around which is a subtle rainbow (cf. Rev 4:3). Not subtle, however, is the Christological design of Brumidi's work.[15]

15. It is notable that a self-identified Christian and nationalist such as Rich Lowry acknowledges this combination of Christological and pagan aspects of this painted depiction of Washington, yet does not seem to have a problem with such an overtly religious depiction. Lowry, *The Case for Nationalism,* 19.

However, while the nationalist doctrines of resurrection and ascension are parasitically dependent upon Christian theology, the differences between the Christian and nationalist conceptions of these doctrines are pronounced in stark relief. In Christianity, Christ's ascension is a "necessary complement and completion of the resurrection."[16] In nationalism, apotheosis can only follow the very permanent death of a merely human ruler.

16. Berkhof, *Systematic Theology*, 350.

14

THE SPIRIT AND THE BRIDE

I BELIEVE IN THE HOLY SPIRIT

Christians believe that God the Father ordains redemption, God the Son accomplishes redemption, and God the Holy Spirit applies redemption. As a member of the Trinity, the Holy Spirit, known also as "the Spirit" or "Spirit of God," is a unique person of the Godhead who fills and indwells the people of God (Rom 8:11; Eph 5:18; 2 Tim 1:14), and binds the church together in unity (Eph 4:1–6; Phil 2:1–4). Moreover, the New Testament emphasizes the Spirit's role actively leading and guiding Christians: "When the Spirit of truth comes, he will guide you into all the truth, for he will not speak on his own authority, but whatever he hears he will speak, and he will declare to you the things that are to come" (John 16:13).

Nationalism seems to convey its own doctrine of the Holy Spirit by speaking of a spirit (or spirits) that may unify, guide, and inspire the people of a nation. As already referenced in chapter 3, French nationalist Ernest Renan writes that "A nation is a soul, a spiritual principle."[1] So too, Joseph Stalin seems to suggest a part of a nation's essence resides in a common "psychological make-up or, as it otherwise called, 'national character,'" which was

1. Renan, *Qu'est-ce qu'une nation?*, 26.

"intangible to the observer," but "manifested" in a distinctive common culture.[2] As a staunch materialist, Stalin could never deign to use a term like "spirit," yet his conception of the nation conveys a clearly spiritual element. Using the Pauline language of "powers," Hendrik Berkhof describes, from personal experience in Nazi Germany, how the spiritual forces of nationalism can be tangibly felt:

> When Hitler took the helm in Germany in 1933, the Powers of *Volk*, race, and state took a new grip on men. Thousands were grateful, after the confusion of the preceding years, to find their lives again protected from chaos, order and security restored. No one could withhold himself, without utmost effort, from the grasp these Powers had on men's inner and outer life. While studying in Berlin (1937) I myself experienced almost literally how such Powers may be "in the air." . . . . They acted as if they were ultimate values, calling for loyalty as if they were the gods of the cosmos.[3]

This "national spirit" (*Volkgeist*) may also speak in and through the will of the people of the nation.[4] This naturally leads the nation to adopt laws and documents that either explicitly or implicitly are understood as "inspired" (cf. 2 Tim 3:16).[5] Thus, the ancient Code of Hammurabi depicts the king standing before the Shamash, the sun god, receiving the words of the law, which possess a sense of divine authority, deriving from divine inspiration.[6]

2. Hutchinson and Anthony D. Smith, *Nationalism*, 20.

3. Berkhof, *Christ and the Powers*, 32.

4. Smith, *Nationalism*, 42.

5. Lowry, *The Case for Nationalism*, 22.

6. "The Code of Hammurabi." In *ANET* 163–180.

The Code of Hammurabi, King of Babylon, 1792–1750 B.C.E. Relief on basalt. The Louvre, Paris. Photograph courtesy of Gary Lee Todd.

So too, even in the modern era, some have characterized the United States Constitution as inspired.[7]

However, in distinction from the Holy Spirit, who brings peace (John 14:26–27), liberty (2 Cor 3:17), and life (Rom 8:6), the spirit(s) of nationalism bring forth unity and power, yes; but also, war and enslavement. The spirit of nationalism can even demand human sacrifice when necessary. As Renan opines, "A great aggregation of men, with a healthy spirit and warmth of heart, creates a moral conscience which is called a nation. When this moral conscience proves its strength by sacrifices that demand abdication of the individual for the benefit of the community, it is legitimate and has the right to exist."[8] These words are spoken with a romantic

---

7. Whitehead and Perry, *Taking America Back for God,* xi.

8. Renan, *Qu'est-ce qu'une nation?,* 26.

idealism that can hauntingly inspire a nation both to bring forth the beauty of the Eiffel Tower as well as the Reign of Terror.

THE HOLY CATHOLIC CHURCH, THE COMMUNION OF THE SAINTS

In Christian dogmatics, the doctrine of the church organically flows from the doctrine of the Spirit. The church is the body of Christ, filled with the Spirit of Christ, called to continue the mission of Christ. As the people of God, the church is also the new temple in which the Spirit of God resides. As Paul reminds the Christians of Ephesus: "So then you are no longer strangers and aliens, but you are fellow citizens with the saints and members of the household of God, built on the foundation of the apostles and prophets, Christ Jesus himself being the cornerstone, in whom the whole structure, being joined together, grows into a holy temple in the Lord. In him you also are being built together into a dwelling place for God by the Spirit" (Eph 2:19–22).

In imitation of this Christian relationship between the Holy Spirit and the church, nationalism seeks to create a similar relationship between the spirit(s) of the nation and the people of the nation. For this reason, the territory of a nation is often understood as a being inhabited by the spirit, power, and moral qualities of its inhabitants. Grosby notes:

> The modern nation is recognized by its members as being more than a merely spatial setting—a house—for the random interaction between individuals. It is viewed as a home, where the 'spirit' of the past and current generations has filled up that spatial setting, making it a homeland, a territory. This spirit of past and current generations are those traditions that contribute to organizing an area of space into a territory and that, as such, provide meaning around which the territorial relation is organized.[9]

---

9. Grosby, *Nationalism*, 46.

Nationalism may also mimic the doctrine of the church by construing the nation as a "chosen people" who are covenantally bound and entrusted with a divine sense of mission.[10] This tendency is most particularly evidenced in nationalisms of western, Christianized nations that intentionally create connections between their respective nations and Israel of the Old Testament. For example, David T. Koyzis observes that many conservative evangelicals in the United States, "who are otherwise fairly literal in their interpretation of Scripture . . . see their own American nation as the potential beneficiary [of Old Testament Israel's covenantal] promises."[11] One example of this tendency is the common application of 2 Chronicles 7:14 to the American nation. 2 Chronicles 7:14 reads: "if my people who are called by my name humble themselves, and pray and seek my face and turn from their wicked ways, then I will hear from heaven and will forgive their sin and heal their land." The immediate context of this oft-quoted verse concerns the dedication of King Solomon's temple and a charge to the people of Israel to diligently keep the terms of Israel's covenant with Yahweh, according to the standards of the Old Testament law (Deuteronomy 28 is particularly in view). The broader historical context of 2 Chronicles suggests that the reading audience was composed of the Jewish people who were returning from exile. In other words, 2 Chronicles 7:14 was a charge to ancient Israel to remember and renew their covenant with God. To apply this verse to the United States—a nation that does not have a covenant with God based on the Old Testament law—is an irresponsible exegetical fallacy.

Nevertheless, the temptation to envision the American nation through the lens of Old Testament Israel is a powerful and effective trope for American nationalist thinking. In his book *The Case for Nationalism*, Rich Lowry (a self-identified Christian and nationalist) explicitly argues for viewing ancient Israel as the quintessential model of nationhood and nationalism. In a portrait of Jewish nationalism that should confound the discerning Christian reader,

10. Smith, *Chosen Peoples*, 7.

11. Koyzis, *Political Visions and Illusions*, 116.

he even uses the Bar Kokhba Revolt (132–136 A.D.) against Rome as a positive example of nationalist sentiment.[12] This characterization is an odd choice for a few reasons. Firstly, the Bar Kokhba revolt ended in definitively disastrous results for the Jewish people, including over half a million deaths and widespread depopulation of Judean territory. But even more disturbing, in leading this rebellion, Simon bar Kokhba intentionally presented himself as the messiah.[13] In other words, Bar Kokhba was a literal anti-Christ, who led himself, his followers, and his people into death with his nationalist vision.[14]

However, the temptation to equate a given nation with ancient Israel, or even to view a given nation as the continuation of ancient Israel, is not unique the United States. In the period following the Dutch War of Independence (1566–1648), the Dutch people were often understood as a new Israel, with Holland as a new Jerusalem, and William the Silent as a new King David.[15] Reflecting this mentality, Dutch poet Adriaan Valerius penned this concluding prayer in his "The Netherlands Anthem of Commemoration": "O Lord when all was ill with us You brought us up into a land wherein we were enriched through trade and commerce and have dealt kindly with us, even as you have the Children of Israel from their Babylonian prison; the waters receded before us and you brought us dry-footed even as the people of yore, with Moses and with Joshua,

---

12. Lowry, *The Case for Nationalism*, 67–70.

13. Bar Kokhba's given name was Simon ben Koseva. He was later called "Bar Kokhba" by Rabbi Akiva, a popular and influential religious figure. The title "Bar Kokhba" (meaning son of a star) is a reference to the prophecy of Numbers 24:17 which was often associated with messianic hope: "I see him, but not now; I behold him, but not near: a *star* shall come out of Jacob, and a scepter shall rise out of Israel; it shall crush the forehead of Moab and break down all the sons of Sheth" (emphasis mine). Thus, while he did not technically declare himself to be the messiah, Bar Kokhba eagerly embraced and appropriated the title.

14. In another bizarre move, Lowry seems to depict the period of the Judges—a period in biblical history universally recognized as a downward spiral—as a parallel and precursor to popular rule and modern nationalism. Lowry, *The Case for Nationalism*, 70.

15. Smith, *Chosen Peoples*, 46.

were brought to their Promised Land."[16] In a similar vein, English courtier John Lyly proclaims of his nation, "So tender a care hath he always had of that England, as of a new Israel, his chosen and peculiar people."[17]

Characterization of the nation as a chosen people is further developed in the religious and liturgical practices that surround the religion of nationalism. After all, the cult of the nation requires a cultic community and practices that cultivate that community. As Philosopher James K.A. Smith has argued, ritual practices play a pivotal role in spiritual formation: "This formation happens liturgically, not didactically; that is, such rituals grab hold of our desire and our love through our bodies—through material, visceral rhythms, images, and experiences that subtly inscribe in us a desire for other kingdoms."[18] Thus, daily practices (like pledging allegiance to the flag), weekly practices (like singing the National Anthem at a high school football game), and annual practices (like a Fourth of July parade) can be understood as nationalist versions of historic Christian practices of worship (daily prayer, weekly corporate worship, and annual feast days).[19] Hayes will go so far as to suggest that most American national holidays function in the same ways as traditional holidays on the Christian liturgical calendar: " . . . the Fourth of July is a nationalist Christmas, Flag Day an adaptation of Corpus Christi, . . . Veterans Day a patriotic version of All Souls Day, while in imitation of the saints' days . . . are observed the birthdays of national saints and heroes, such as Washington and Lincoln."[20]

However, if nationalism is able to successfully portray the nation as a chosen people and a covenant community through liturgical practices, it inevitably must practice a form of excommunication in order to maintain that distinctive identity. Thus, if nationalism takes on a mode of ethnic nationalism, the nation

16. Smith, *Chosen Peoples*, 46.
17. John Lyly, *Complete Works*, 205.
18. Smith, *Desiring the Kingdom*, 104.
19. Smith, *Desiring the Kingdom*, 104–105.
20. Hayes, *Nationalism*, 167.

will inevitably be drawn toward the practice of ethnic exclusion, or even the horror of ethnic cleansing. The Armenian genocide by the hands of Ottoman Turks, the Jewish Holocaust by the hands of German Nazis, or the contemporary subjugation of the Uighur people group at the hands of the Chinese Communist Party each represent a nationalist perversion of the doctrine of excommunication.[21] If, on the other hand, nationalism takes on a more civic mode, citizens who dare to question, critique, or dissent from ideological orthodoxy will be declared traitors and heretics, and thereby cast out of the communion of the nation.[22]

In light of this analysis, when a nation, state government, or political party becomes beholden to a spirit of nationalism, it ceases to be a merely sociological entity or human institution and transforms into something more like a church. More directly stated, when a group of people becomes ideologically possessed by nationalism, it becomes a *false* church.

21. See the chapter on "Nationalist Imperialism and Intolerance" in Hayes, *Nationalism*, 94–115.

22. Koyzis, *Political Visions and Illusions*, 109.

15

JUSTIFICATION AND JUDGMENT

THE FORGIVENESS OF SINS

For the Christian, forgiveness is found in confession, repentance, and, most importantly, faith in Christ Jesus (1 John 1:9; Acts 2:38; 13:38–39; Eph 1:7). At the cross, Jesus was imputed with the sins of his people, so that his people might be imputed with his righteousness (2 Cor 5:21). This imputation of righteousness has been historically understood by Protestant Christians as the doctrine of justification. A cornerstone of Pauline theology is the notion that this justification comes by faith in Christ (Rom 3:29; 5:1; Gal 2:16, 3:24; Phil 3:9). Thus, while Christians rightly value good works that come from a heart transformed by saving faith, justification itself comes only by faith, not by works. But whereas a Christian understanding of justification is founded on faith in Christ, a nationalist understanding of justification is founded on one's faithfulness to the nation.

In this way, the nationalist rendering of justification is an unapologetically utilitarian enterprise by which the ends of nationalism quite literally *justify* the means. Fraud, theft, espionage, assassination, and war crimes, while objectively evil actions, may be pardoned if forgiveness of the offending party is deemed expedient for the nation's interests.[1]

It was, thus, for nationalist—not Christian—sympathies that Pope Pius XI praised Benito Mussolini as a "man sent by providence."[2] While the fascist Italian dictator was far from a model Catholic, and even viewed the state as superior to the church, the Pope found Mussolini's opposition to communism and traditional liberalism to be in the best interest of both the Vatican and the Italian nation. Similarly, many theologically conservative Protestants in Germany were willing to ignore the Nazi's anti-Semitism and pagan aspects because they believed Hitler's anti-communism was of paramount national importance.

Sadly, professed Christians can adopt a nationalist understanding of justification, even as it relates to Christian salvation. In 1980, after the election of U.S. President Ronald Reagan, a Methodist Bishop announced, "The blame [for Reagan's victory] ought not to be placed on all the vigor of the Right, but maybe weakness of the saints . . . [a better day will come] if the people of faith will be strengthened by defeat and address themselves to the new agenda upon us."[3] In a similar way, during the 2020 U.S. presidential election, Pastor John MacArthur told then President Donald Trump during a phone call, "any real, true believer is going to be on your side in this election."[4] In both of these examples, Christian pastors effectively treat belief in a political ideology—not faith in Christ—as the determinative issue regarding whether or not a person is a part of "the people of faith" and a "real, true believer."

---

1. Bomboy, "Presidential pardons: a constitutional and historical review," https://constitutioncenter.org/blog/presidential-pardons-a-constitutional-and-historical-review

2. Pierard, "An Age of Ideology." In *Introduction to the History of Christianity* 588.

3. Colson, "The Power Illusion." In *Power Religion*, 37.

4. Gryboski, "John MacArthur says 'true believers will vote for Trump, can't affirm abortion and trans activism," https://www.christianpost.com/news/john-macarthur-says-true-believers-will-vote-for-trump-cant-affirm-abortion-and-trans-activism.html

THE RESURRECTION OF THE BODY
AND THE LIFE EVERLASTING

The Christian gospel is a gospel of ultimate and final hope. The kingdom of God that has been inaugurated in the first coming of Jesus Christ will find its complete consummation in his glorious return, in which all the brokenness of God's sin-fractured creation will be healed. As the Apostle John proclaims, "He will wipe away every tear from their eyes, and death shall be no more, neither shall there be mourning, nor crying, nor pain anymore, for the former things have passed away" (Rev 21:4). More than a potential or probable outcome for God's people, this promise of restoration is "trustworthy and true" (22:6), for the resurrected and ascended Christ himself testifies, "Surely I am coming soon" (22:20a). Thus, the eschatological hope of the New Testament is an unflinchingly *certain* hope for which Christians cry out, "Amen. Come, Lord Jesus!" (22:20b).

Nationalism too possesses an eschatology, for, like the Christian church, the nation is understood by nationalism as an eschatological community. Anthony D. Smith explains:

> The nation, in the eyes of nationalists, can be described as a community of history and destiny, or better, a community in which history requires or produces destiny—a particular national destiny. This idea of *destiny* carries far more emotional freight than notions of the future. Destinies are determined by histories; destinies chart a unique course and fate; destinies speak of transcendence, perhaps immortality; for we "live on" in the memory and judgment of posterity.[5]

Note that Smith connects nationalism's sense of eschatology, or "destiny," with providing an avenue through which members of a nation may acquire a type of resurrected "immortality" within the historical memory of future generations. From the ideas of the "Third Reich" to "Manifest Destiny," nationalism offers a vision of

5. Smith, *Nationalism*, 33.

a glorious future in which its adherents may find an immanentized version of "life everlasting."

The *Aeneid* provides yet another vivid example of this nationalist doctrine at work. Just before his final and decisive battle, by which he will lay claim to his promised bride and promised homeland, Aeneas is given a dazzling set of new armor by his divine mother. Venus commissioned the work from Vulcan, god of fire and maker of armor for the Olympian gods, on behalf of her war-sieged son. While this virtually indestructible armor certainly serves a *function* in battle, it is the *form* of the martial equipment, namely the shield, that is most significant. For emblazoned in *bas relief* upon this shield, "the Lord of fire, knowing the prophets, knowing the age to come, had wrought the future story of Italy, the triumphs of the Romans."[6] The shield visually recounts the tales of Romulus and Remus, the founding of the Roman republic, the travails of the Punic Wars, all culminating with Octavian's victory over Mark Antony and Cleopatra at Actium in 31 B.C. The final scene portrayed is of the triumphant Octavian (now Caesar Augustus) riding into Rome in victorious procession and festal joy. In a description remarkably similar to Psalm 68 and Ephesians 4,[7] the conquering king rides into the Eternal City bearing a host of captives: "Conquered races passed along in long procession, varied in languages as in their dress and arms. Here Mulciber, divine smith, had portrayed the Nomad tribes and Afri with ungirded flowing robes, here Leleges and Carians, and here Gelonians with quivers."[8] It is with this glorious vision of the future before him that Aeneas, the "man at war,"[9] will wage his warfare. It is with similar visions of future glory that nationalism has inspired generations of mankind and nations.

Yet, in contrast to the Christian hope of New Creation, which is guaranteed by God and brought into being by the Son of Man,

6. Virgil, *The Aeneid*, bk. 8, lines 848–851.

7. See previous discussions on Psalm 68 and Ephesians 4 in chapters 7 and 9 respectively.

8. Virgil, *The Aeneid*, bk. 8, lines 976–982.

9. Virgil, *The Aeneid*, bk. 1, line 1.

the hope of nationalism is a reality ushered in only by the work of man. As with the doctrine of salvation, the eschatology of nationalism is a fundamentally Pelagian and this-worldly endeavor, and, therefore, a highly contingent and transitory hope. For this reason, Renan warns, "Nations are not something eternal. They have begun, they will end."[10] The nationalist, then, must consistently make the appropriate sacrifices necessary to maintain the nation and secure its future hope. Arguing for the pragmatic virtues of nationalism, R.R. Reno contends, "We must attend the strong gods [one of which he explicitly identifies as nationalism] who come from above and animate the best of our traditions. Only that kind of leadership will forestall the return of the dark gods who rise up from below."[11]

One salient consequence of nationalist eschatology is that it tends to functionally replace traditional religion with politics. If one political party is animated by one form of ideological nationalism and another party is animated by an opposing form of ideological nationalism, every political contest will necessarily take on an apocalyptic and cosmic import. If the right party acquires power, it will bring forth a New Heavens and a New Earth. If the wrong party acquires power, it will bring forth Ragnarök. Since either future is always on the cusp of arrival, for the nationalist, there can be no rest or blessed assurance, as there can be for the Christian. Instead, with constant religious fervor and vigilance, the nationalist must heed the words of Ghanan President Kwame Nkrumah, "Seek ye first the political kingdom, and all things shall be added to you."[12]

A DIFFERENT GOSPEL

For virtually every core component of Christian theology, nationalism offers a corresponding but distinctly contrary doctrine. As a

10. Renan, *Qu'est-ce qu'une nation?*, 26.

11. Reno, *The Return of the Strong Gods*, 162.

12. Smith, *Chosen Peoples*, 10.

demonically empowered ideology, nationalism is a different gospel; a false gospel.

Nationalism often employs the language of Christians, appeals to the sensibilities of Christians, and even offers security from the perceived threats made against Christians. For this reason, many Christians have historically fallen prey to the influence of nationalist doctrine. Yet, something like contemporary Christian nationalism in the United States is nothing more than one manifestation of an ancient and demonically charged form of idolatry.

Christian nationalism engenders a political allegiance that must supersede all other loyalties. It casts political leaders as messianic figures. It turns political opinions into the only "good news" that adherents are willing to share with their neighbors. It places eschatological hope within the kings and kingdoms of this world. Christian nationalism creates a religion complete with leaders, practices, and self-defined orthodox beliefs. But it is a religion that is incompatible with biblical Christianity. In sum, all forms of nationalism—including Christian nationalism—preach a different gospel, and as the Apostle Paul declares, " . . . even if we or an angel from heaven should preach to you a gospel contrary to the one we preached to you, let him be accursed" (Gal 1:8).

Make no mistake: the term "Christian nationalist" is just as oxymoronic as "Yahwist Baal worshiper." When Christianity mixes with nationalism, the sum of this syncretism yields only nationalism. Light has no fellowship with darkness, Christ has no accord with Belial, and the temple of God has no agreement with idols (2 Cor 6:15–16). For this reason, Christians must have no part in nationalism.

Part V

WHERE DO WE GO FROM HERE?

16

CONTENDING WITH FALSE GOSPELS

CONFRONTING NATIONALISM

What are the practical implications of the preceding study for pastors and Christian leaders? While it may take another book to answer that question thoroughly, in this brief section, I would like to provide a brief sketch of a way forward.

Christian pastors have been entrusted with the sacred task of preaching the gospel of Jesus Christ. Inherent in this call is the mandate to oppose and expose false gospels. The biblical and theological analyses of the previous chapters have shown how nationalism is a false gospel that is both ancient and demonic. As such, nationalism must be named, critiqued, and renounced every bit as much as any other false gospel.

In this chapter, 2 Timothy 4:1–2 will provide a framework for confronting nationalism as a false gospel: "I charge you in the presence of God and of Christ Jesus, who is to judge the living and the dead, and by his appearing and his kingdom: preach the word; be ready in season and out of season; reprove, rebuke, and exhort, with complete patience and teaching" (2 Tim 4:1–2).

PREACH THE WORD

Christian pastors are to be ambassadors of the kingdom of God, not lobbyists for the kingdom of men. We are to be prophets, not puppets. When cultural pressures tempt the stewards of the mysteries of God to placate and pacify the powers from the pulpit, we must choose to fear Christ—the resurrected, ascended, and soon-returning Lord—above the fear of men (cf. Prov 29:25). For this reason, Paul charges Timothy "in the presence of God and of Christ Jesus, who is to judge the living and the dead, and by his appearing and his kingdom . . . [to] preach the word" (2 Tim 4:1–2a).

The power of Christ is infinitely greater than the spiritual rulers of this age. This truth must be an ever-present, living reality in the minds and hearts of Christian preachers, for the proclamation of the gospel is itself a confrontation with and contradiction of the powers. The coming kingdom of God necessitates the terminus of all kingdoms of men, and, against this coming reality, the nations will rage and set themselves against the LORD and his Anointed (Ps 2:1–2). Knowing this, pastors must be bold and courageous to allow the authoritative, God-breathed words of Scripture to set the agenda of the church's pulpit, not the partisan talking points of political ideologies. Even when the itching ears of some seek for pastors to weaponize their sermons in advancement of a nationalist agenda, the sole aim and ambition of the pastor must be to please God (2 Cor 5:9).

BE READY IN SEASON AND OUT OF SEASON

In preaching the word, Timothy must also "be ready in season and out of season." The term "be ready" (*epistēthi*)[1] means to actively and urgently "take a stand."[2] This posture of vigilance is necessary "in season" and "out of season"; in convenient times and inconvenient times. The broader context of this passage suggests

1. Interestingly, the word "*epistēthi*" comes from the Greek root "*istēmi*," which also appears four times in Ephesians 6:10–20.

2. Spencer, 2 *Timothy and Titus*, 135.

the reason for this call to vigilance lies in the ever-present threat of false teaching that seeks to infiltrate Timothy's congregation.

Part IV of this book illustrates how nationalism bears its own demonically inspired false gospel. Even more, this false gospel (in its legion of variegated forms) currently pervades every cable news station, every social media platform, and a host of written sources. Sometimes, sadly, nationalism is even eagerly proclaimed from church pulpits in the veneer of Christ's name. Thus, it is paramount for pastors to practice prayerful spiritual discernment (cf. 1 John 4:1–6). We must be subject to the Spirit of God, not the spirit of the age or the nationalist spirit of any political party. As C.S. Lewis once quipped, "The demon inherent in every political party is at all times ready enough to disguise himself as the Holy Ghost."[3]

Instead of parroting political rhetoric, the church must prophetically speak to this situation. The shepherds of God's sheep must not boldly denounce the false idols of money and sex while remaining silent when people deify their nation or political ideology. Christian leaders have a responsibility to wisely, strategically, and directly contend with nationalism through preaching, teaching, publishing, and the discipleship ministries of the church. Moreover, the kingdom of God must be proclaimed in a way that shows how the gospel of Jesus Christ is *better* than the false gospel of nationalism. Pastors must proactively catechize their parishioners against the siren calls of nationalism, or else political pundits and grifter politicians will gladly step into that void and disciple the people of God into this false gospel.

REPROVE AND REBUKE

The command to "reprove" and "rebuke" relates to exposing and correcting sinful behavior. As it relates to nationalism, this may include pastors calling attention to the way that proponents of nationalism utilize religious or even scriptural language in proselytizing their views.

---

3. Lewis, "Meditation on the Third Commandment," 198.

Reproving and rebuking nationalism may also take the form of correcting congregation members for words or behaviors that are encouraged by nationalism but are unbecoming of Christians. For example, nationalism often tempts people to vilify and demonize those who disagree with their political views in impersonal, online venues such as social media platforms.

Social media is by no means intentionally evil. Nevertheless, it has provided fearful and frustrated people with an avenue to unleash venomous words upon one another in a way that should grieve Christians. Because social media algorithms often value the controversial, the provocative, and the incendiary, social media often unconsciously lures users toward a destructive form of discourse. In this environment, people are tempted to arrogantly proclaim the rightness of their own views with bravado and pride, often misrepresenting and impugning the motives of those with whom they disagree. However, using words in this worldly manner way is unwise, unproductive, and unchristian. It is walking as the gentiles do (Eph 4:17).

To this behavior, pastors must train their congregations to know that the Christian manner of life is not modeled after the powers of this world. The Christian manner of life is modeled after Christ, who loved us while we were his enemies (cf. Rom 5:10). Christians must show that same grace to the world, so that in us, they might see the grace of Christ. We must speak words of grace, so that in our voice, the world hears the gracious voice of Christ. When Christians bear witness to Christ, how we speak matters. Our manner must not contradict our message.

EXHORT

The command to "exhort" relates to that toward which pastors are calling their parishioners. It is not enough to warn Christians *against* nationalism. We must also call the people of God *toward* the aspects of the Christian gospel that directly challenge the false gospel of nationalism. Some particularly important hortatory points of emphasis include: exilic identity and allegiance, godly submission with appropriate suspicion, racial reconciliation, and a politics of eternal hope.

Exilic Identity and Allegiance

Christians must be exhorted to embrace the identity of "elect exiles" (1 Pet 1:1). As the Jewish captives in Babylonia were to understand their call to live in a land not their own (cf. Jer 29:4–14), so too the people of God today are called to be in the world, but not of it (cf. John 17:14 –17). As "elect exiles," Christians possess a dual calling of preserving our distinctiveness from culture while at the same time being culturally engaged in ministry.

Moreover, our identity determines our allegiance. For Christians, our ultimate loyalty must be to our God and his kingdom—not our nationality, not our political team, not our ideological tribe. As Paul says, "But our citizenship is in heaven, and from it we await a Savior, the Lord Jesus Christ" (Phil 3:20). Baptism is thus a statement of Christian identity and allegiance against the powers, proclaiming that we—no matter our ethnic heritage—are no longer under their dominion or beholden to their claims (Col 2:11–15). For this reason, Basil the Great attests that the "renouncing Satan and his angels" as part of the baptismal creed is a practice going back to the apostles themselves.[4] Moreover, every time we pray, "Your kingdom come" (Matt 6:10), we reaffirm our loyalty to a true and better nation and renounce the powers of darkness by pleading for their reign to come to a consummated end.

Godly Submission with Appropriate Suspicion

Scripture envisions state governments that belong to nations as a legitimate source of authority designed and appointed by God to restrain evil and promote justice (Rom 13:1–7). Even pagan governments serve a common grace function in the lives of individuals and communities. For this reason, Christians must be exhorted

---

4. Basil of Caesarea, "The Book of Saint Basil on the Spirit," ch. 27, sec. 66.

to "be subject to" (Rom 13:1: 1 Pet 2:13), "honor" (Rom 13:7; 1 Pet 2:17), and even make "supplications, prayers, intercessions, and thanksgiving" for governmental leaders like "kings and all who are in high positions" (1 Tim 2:1–2). Thus, Scripture calls for a posture of humble, voluntary submission to the governmental authorities of nations, as a way of honoring and submitting to the sovereign authority of God (Rom 13:1).

Yet, Scripture does not call for uncritical compliance on behalf of the people of God to all leaders. The Apostle Peter explicitly says in Acts 5:29, there are times in which Christians "must obey God rather than man." Governmental leaders may demand for Christians to sin against God, for example, by forbidding gospel proclamation (as the mandates of the Sanhedrin in Acts 5) or requiring the worship of the nation (as in compelled participation in the Roman imperial cult). In such instances, it is both right and necessary for pastors to boldly speak truth to the powers and lead Christians into a godly resistance to the authority of men for the sake of obeying the higher authority of the Lord Jesus.

Thus, while Romans 13 teaches that state governments can be tools in God's hand to promote justice and restrain sin, Revelation 13 teaches that those same state governments can turn into "beasts" that violently oppose the kingdom of God (Rev 13; cf. Dan 7:1–8). Christians will be less likely to fall prey to the deception of nationalism if they are exhorted to live in tension between Romans 13 and Revelation 13; between godly submission to and appropriate suspicion of the "earthly city."[5]

Racial Reconciliation

Nationalism often manifests in the form of "ethnic nationalism"; that is, a form of nationalism that is centered around ethnic or

---

5. "Accordingly, two cities have been formed by two loves: the earthly by the love of self, even to the contempt of God; the heavenly by the love of God, even to the contempt of self. The former, in a word, glories in itself, the latter in the Lord." Augustine of Hippo, "The City of God," bk. 14, ch. 28.

racial identity.[6] From the time of God's judgment on Babel in Genesis 11, the spiritual powers that fuel ethnic nationalism have led the various peoples of the world into confusion, division, hostility, and the destructive and deadly force of racism (cf. Deut 32:8). However, out of the nations, God called Abram to father a family destined to become a divinely chosen nation. Through the "offspring" of Abram (Abraham), "all the families of the earth shall be blessed" (Gen 12:3).

Jesus Christ is the "offspring" of Abraham in who the covenants of God find their fulfillment and fruition (Gal 3:16). Through Christ, in whom "there is neither Jew nor Greek" (Gal 3:28), ethnic gentiles may also inherit the "blessing of Abraham" (Gal 3:14). Any claim that the powers once had upon the nations has been canceled by the cross of Jesus Christ, by which "[God] disarmed the rulers and authorities and put them to open shame, by triumphing over them in [Christ]" (Col 2:15). For Christians, the curse of Babel is reversed and the reconciled reality of Pentecost has come.

Thus, in an indicative sense believing Jews and gentiles—and, indeed, all Christians of all ethnicities—have been reconciled as "one in Christ" (Eph 2:16; Gal 3:28). Yet, the church must be exhorted to actively appropriate, preserve, and "walk in" the miraculous unity that Christ has created for his people (Eph 4:1–6).[7] Moreover, when the Christians fail to "walk in" in this reality, and instead fall back into the old fleshly ways of racism and ethnic nationalism, we must confess our sins and repent, both individually and collectively.[8] When we recognize the ways we have sinned against one another in the past and in the present, we must not succumb to the worldly temptation of defensiveness nor the malaise of indifference. Instead, we must call one another toward justice,

---

6. Smith, *Nationalism*, 43–45.

7. Darko, *Against Powers and* Principalities, 118.

8. See for example the prayers of corporate confession and repentance in Nehemiah 1:5–11 and Daniel 9:3–19.

righteousness, and humility—even when repentance is difficult and costly.[9]

Nevertheless, when the "mystery" of the gentile inclusion into God's covenant people is tangibly displayed through humble unity and reconciliation within the church, it is a spiritually charged manifestation of the wisdom of God "to the rulers and authorities in the heavenly places" (Eph 3:10). Even more, when the church embodies the reality of gospel-empowered racial reconciliation, it offers a watching world—a world that groans with racial division and the failed worldly measures to heal that division—a previewed glimpse of a day to come when God will gather people of all nations into the new Jerusalem (cf. Rev 21:22–27).

A Politics of Eternal Hope

In an increasingly secular age, many people feel a level of alienation, powerlessness, and hopelessness as it relates to the political landscape. However, in such a context, Christians must be exhorted to bear a counter-cultural witness to the ultimate hope we share in the coming kingdom of Christ. Pastors must renounce a worldly, utilitarian, nationalist form of political engagement wherein we exclusively promote our own self-interest and use government as a club to beat our group's agenda into society. This approach will only contribute to a vicious cycle of action and reaction; of vengeance and resentment.

Rather, Christians are to "seek the welfare" and the common good of our here and now, but always with eternity in view (Jer 29:7). No matter the political situation within the kingdom of man, we are called to possess an unflinching hope that God will ultimately bring about good for his people. We will face struggles and challenges, but restoration is coming. For Christians, our

---

9. See for example Paul's confrontation of Peter in Galatians 2:11–21. One might find a modern parallels of such Christian to Christian confrontations in the Jemar Tisby's *The Color of Compromise* and Duke L. Kwon and Gregory Thompson's *Reparations*.

ultimate hope is not in a restored America (or any nation for that matter), but in a restored creation (cf. Rev 21:4).

Whatever our political opinions might be, all political systems are stained by sin and corruption, and thus doomed to end. All Babylons and the powers behind them will fall (cf. Rev 18). Thus, Christians must embrace the liberating truth that politics are, at their very best, a necessary coping mechanism for navigating justice in a fallen world. Politics may be good and useful, but they can never be ultimate. They cannot save us, and they can never be our hope. Over against nationalist temptation to ascribe spiritual ultimacy to politics, pastors must exhort their congregations toward the salvation and ultimate hope that lies only in Christ and his kingdom.

WITH PATIENCE AND TEACHING

A final aspect of Paul's counsel in 2 Timothy 4:1–2, related to the preaching ministry of the church and contending with false gospels, lies in the command to "preach the word . . . with patience and teaching" (2 Tim 4:2).

Ministers should not expect nationalism, or any other false gospel, to be definitively rooted out by a single sermon, pastoral conversation, or blog post. Pastoral ministry is a patient enterprise. The teaching ministry of the church is most fruitful when congregation members are regularly exposed to the faithful teaching of God's word, which does not return void and brings forth maturity (Isa 55:11; Col 1:28). Like weeds in a garden that arise from wind-blown seeds, false doctrines will sprout up in Christian congregations through the influence of popular teachers, ideologues, and cultural circumstances. Thus, pastors should seek to correct false doctrine in a way that is appropriately clear, direct, and bold; all the while being mindful that it is through *patience* that some will hear the word of God, hold it fast in an honest and good heart, and bear fruit (Luke 8:15).

At the same time, pastors should seek to avoid unnecessary offense. True, the gospel of Jesus Christ will inevitably be a "stone of stumbling, and a rock of offense" (1 Pet 2:8) for unregenerate hearers, no matter how winsome and gentle the messenger. With this said, we must also recognize the real difference between the gospel causing offense and a preacher (or believer!) of the gospel causing offense.

As Proverbs 12:18 teaches, "There is one whose rash words are like sword thrusts, but the tongue of the wise brings healing." When dealing with a false doctrine as cancerous and deceptive as nationalism, pastors need to forge their words into surgical scalpels of patience and persuasion instead of blunt axes of condescending insult and beratement.

However, to preach against nationalism at all is to preach against the powers themselves, and when these powers are attacked, they tend to fight back with a vengeance. How then do we engage in this spiritual war? That topic is the focus of the next chapter.

17

CONTENDING WITH THE POWERS

WE DO NOT WRESTLE AGAINST FLESH AND BLOOD

Whereas the previous chapter explored 2 Timothy 4:1–2 as a model for contending with the doctrines of nationalism, Ephesians 6:10–20 will provide a framework for engaging the spiritual powers that stand behind nationalism:

> Finally, be strong in the Lord and in the strength of his might. Put on the whole armor of God, that you may be able to stand against the schemes of the devil. For we do not wrestle against flesh and blood, but against the rulers, against the authorities, against the cosmic powers over this present darkness, against the spiritual forces of evil in the heavenly places. Therefore take up the whole armor of God, that you may be able to withstand in the evil day, and having done all, to stand firm. Stand therefore, having fastened on the belt of truth, and having put on the breastplate of righteousness, and, as shoes for your feet, having put on the readiness given by the gospel of peace. In all circumstances take up the shield of faith, with which you can extinguish all the flaming darts of the evil one; and take the helmet of salvation, and the sword of the Spirit, which is the word of God, praying at

all times in the Spirit, with all prayer and supplication. To that end, keep alert with all perseverance, making supplication for all the saints, and also for me, that words may be given to me in opening my mouth boldly to proclaim the mystery of the gospel, for which I am an ambassador in chains, that I may declare it boldly, as I ought to speak.

My central claim throughout this book is that nationalism is not only a form of idolatry; it is also a demonically fueled false gospel that stands in opposition to Christ and his church. Thus, contending with nationalism at any level is nothing less than a provocation of hostile spiritual forces.

In light of this dynamic, it is absolutely crucial for Christian pastors to preach and teach what the Bible has to say about the spiritual nature of reality and the spiritual nature of the church's mission.[1] To willfully ignore or minimize topics like angels, demons, and Satan is to preach a truncated, sub-biblical view of reality. Moreover, if Christians do not understand the powers of darkness, they cannot rightly appreciate the extent of Christian redemption, the profoundly cosmic nature of the church's mission, and the spiritual power of the gospel.

Spiritual war is more real than we often think. However, Scripture shows us that the way we are to participate in this spiritual war is far more practical than we often think. From a biblical perspective, spiritual warfare does not involve magic spells or secret incantations. There are no rituals that need to be performed. You do not need to train on a far-away mountaintop in the mystical art of spiritual ninjutsu or audit a Defense Against the Dark Arts course at the nearest seminary. But you must do one thing—and that is to "stand."

According to Ephesians 6:10–20, to "stand" is the primary way Christians are to contend with the powers. In fact, that the word "stand" (histēmi) or some variation of it is used four times in the first few verses of this passage: "Put on the whole armor of God, that you may be able to *stand* against the schemes of the devil

1. Acolatse's concept of "biblical realism" is helpful in this regard. Acolatse, *Powers, Principalities, and Spirits*, 201.

... Therefore take up the whole armor of God, that you may be able to *withstand* in the evil day, and having done all, to *stand* firm. *Stand* therefore, having fastened on the belt of truth . . . " (Eph 6:11; 13–14; emphasis added).

In calling Christians to "stand," Paul is exhorting believers toward a posture of opposition and active resistance to the influence of the powers. [2] He is exhorting Christians to faithful resilience and determined endurance against spiritual attack. But what does it practically look like to "stand against the schemes of the devil"?

STAND IN CHRIST

Firstly, to "stand" means to stand *in Christ*. This goes against the human-centered notion that spiritual warfare is a task we can do in our own strength and willpower. Paul does not command Christians to be strong in their own strength. He says, "Finally, be strong *in the Lord* and in the strength of *his* might" (6:10; emphasis added). Likewise, he doesn't say take up our armor. He says to take up God's armor.

As previously mentioned in chapters 7 and 9 of this book, Ephesians 6 is not the first instance in Scripture that the armor of God makes an appearance. The first appearance of the armor of God is in Isaiah 59.[3] The context is a vision of God as a mighty warrior, fighting on behalf of his people who are experiencing oppression and injustice:

> Justice is turned back, and righteousness stands far away; for truth has stumbled in the public squares, and uprightness cannot enter. Truth is lacking, and he who departs from evil makes himself a prey. The LORD saw it, and it displeased him that there was no justice. He saw that there was no man, and wondered that there was no one to intercede; then his own arm brought him salvation,

2. BDAG 482.

3. It should be noted that the shield of faith is arguably rooted in Psalm 91:4 ("his faithfulness is a shield"), which may technically be older than Isaiah 59.

and his righteousness upheld him. He put on righteousness as a breastplate, and a helmet of salvation on his head; he put on garments of vengeance for clothing, and wrapped himself in zeal as a cloak (Isa 59:14–17).

Notice that here in Isaiah 59, the armor of God is not something human individuals put on. It is something God puts on as *he* goes to fight battles we could never win for ourselves. So, we might ask, why can Paul say we can now put on God's armor? Because we are united with God in Christ.[4] To put on the armor of God is simply to put on Christ. As Paul says elsewhere: "The night is far gone; the day is at hand. So then let us cast off the works of darkness and put on the armor of light. . . . put on the Lord Jesus Christ . . . " (Rom 13:12–14).

Thus, the first key to spiritual warfare is to trust in the strength of God and rest in the promise of his ultimate triumph over all powers of darkness. We are to stand with endurance, against weariness, discouragement, and hardship, knowing that, in Christ, our final vindication and victory is sure and certain. We are to stand the identity Christ has granted us over against the many identities and loyalties offered to us by the kingdoms of this world.

STAND TOGETHER

Secondly, to "stand" means we are to stand together as the body of Christ. There are five imperative verbs all throughout Ephesians 6:10 –20 that function as commands that Christians are to follow (i.e., "you do this"). In the original Greek, it is clear that every one of these commands in the form of a second person plural imperative verb. However, in proper English, the second person singular pronoun (you) and second person plural pronoun (you) are identical. Thus, it is tempting for modern English readers to individualize the commands of passages like Ephesians 6:10–20

4. Recall, the notion of union with Christ is also a crucial idea earlier in the book of Ephesians 1:3 –14. Thus, as chapter 9 previously observed the theme of the believer's position in Christ forms a conceptual *inclusio* that frames the letter to the Ephesians.

that were originally intended to be read and understood in a corporate sense.

However, Paul is not writing to a group of individuals. He is writing to the church. In other words, Paul is not commanding *you*, the individual, to take up the whole armor of God. Rather, if I may offer a linguistic gift from my native Texas, he is exhorting *y'all* to take up the whole armor of God.

This goes against an individualistic understanding of spiritual warfare. How are we to "be strong"? Together. How do we "take up" and "put on" the armor of God? Together. How do we "stand" firm? Together. The armor of God is found on the body of Christ.

In other words, we must strive to "maintain the unity of the Spirit in the bond of peace" (4:3). Against all attempts of the powers to re-divide the church along the old stoicheic lines of political, cultural, ethnic, and nationalistic loyalties (see the discussion on the stoichea in chapter 8), Christians must intentionally resist these old forms of animosity that associated with life outside of Christ. Instead, the church must seek a Christ-honoring unity through humility, justice, heartfelt repentance, and radical forgiveness.

By his resurrection, Christ has been given all authority in heaven and on earth (Matt 28:18). The claim that the powers once had over the pagan nations has been delegitimized (cf. Deut 32:8; 1 Cor 2:6, 8; Eph 2:1–8; Col 2:15). The church has been commissioned to "make disciples of *all* nations" (Matt 28:19; emphasis added); to announce freedom to those once held in spiritual captivity by the powers, so that they might be saved and included into the body of God's covenant people (cf. Eph 2:11–13, 4:8). In this way, the very existence of the church as a multi-ethnic family of faith is an act of spiritual war against the powers. But we must actively participate in who Christ has called us to be.

STAND IN PRAYER

Finally, to "stand" means we are to stand in prayer. Ephesians 6:18 is an exhortation to pray " . . . at all times in the Spirit, with all prayer and supplication. To that end, keep alert with all perseverance, making supplication for all the saints." In this short verse, Christians are called to pray habitually and consistently. We are called to pray alertly and vigilantly. We are called to pray perseveringly, which means we don't get discouraged when circumstances are not what we want them to be. Rather, we keep praying, and we pray not just for ourselves but also for all the saints, even those of different nationalities and differing political views.

However, for the Christian, our humble prayers should always rest in a hopeful confidence. To be sure, there is a tremendous amount of evil wreaking havoc and division in our world and in the church. Yet, for every day of wearying, disappointing, and heart-breaking pain we may experience in life or in ministry, we draw one day closer to the final day when the vicious reign of the powers is brought to a consummated end. But until that day, we must declare and display the gospel of our crucified King. For it is in that message of weakness that our strength is found and our war is won. As Paul says elsewhere, "For though we walk in the flesh, we are not waging war according to the flesh. For the weapons of our warfare are not of the flesh but have divine power to destroy strongholds" (2 Cor 10:3–4).

18

THE EPIPHANY

" . . . his spirit was provoked within him as he saw that the city was full of idols."

—ACTS 17:16

THE DISTRICT OF A GODDESS NAMED COLUMBIA

It was the late spring of 2021, and the first time I had ever visited my nation's capital. Congress had just gotten out of session. CO-VID protocols were being lessened. Restaurants were opening to full capacity, and some of the Smithsonian museums were beginning to receive guests. Sadly, the Supreme Court, White House, and (of course) the Capitol were all fenced off and closed to tours; a sobering reminder of the events of January 6, 2021. Thankfully, however, the many outdoor memorials that populate the National Mall were freely open to the public.

Beholding these monuments, I felt a sense of deep appreciation for my nation, for the founding fathers, and for the countless soldiers who fought to defend their families and their homeland. I felt thankful for my ancestor James Thompson, a Scottish immigrant and former indentured servant who crossed the Delaware with Washington during the Revolutionary War. I thought of my grandfather, Oris L. Odom, who lost both of his legs in occupied France during World War 2. I felt profoundly grateful that this was my nation and my heritage.

But I also could not help but notice that some of these buildings were designed to evoke more than mere gratitude.

As I ascended up the Lincoln Memorial, I was reminded of another ascent I once took up the Acropolis in Athens, where pagan temples of old once stood. Here in modern America, I saw similar massive marble stones, similar Doric columns, an inner sanctum housing a graven image, and carved words above the statue that explicitly designate this sacred space as a "temple." Every inch of this impressive monument was intentionally designed to elicit a sense of awe, devotion, and *worship* from onlookers and pilgrims alike.

It is crucial for Christians to clearly recognize the distinction between rightly ordered patriotism and idolatrous nationalism; to recognize the difference between gratitude to God for one's nation and the temptation to worship one's nation as a god. None of us are above this temptation. Sadly, the people of God have had a long history of looking to political power for salvation. We have a long history of crying out the name of insurrectionist "Barabbas!" instead of the name of the Prince of Peace, who alone has the power to make all things new.

The powers are real, and they are greedy for our affection. Yet, the exhortation of Joshua 24 still applies to the people of God today. We must put away the gods of our fathers and the gods of the nations. We must choose this day who we will serve.

THE PRAYER OF A WEST TEXAS PASTOR

In contending with nationalism as a pastor, I have tried to show my congregation a vision of God's glory in a world of chaos. I have tried to teach them that when the kings and kingdoms of this world contend for our hope and allegiance, that, as Christians, our ultimate hope and highest allegiance belongs to Christ alone. I have tried to disciple the people I love in what it means to hold the divinely granted identity of "elect exiles."

Sadly, I have experienced heartache and grief when people of both major U.S. political parties have left my congregation because I would not promote their preferred political ideology or amplify partisan echo chambers. But by the grace of God, I have also seen some people grow in faith and fear of the Lord.

Written in the midst of a season of intense political division and a global pandemic, this volume has reminded me that I am most certainly not sufficient for these things in my own strength (2 Cor 2:16). But I sincerely believe the preceding chapters have abundantly shown that what is today commonly referred to as nationalism is an ancient and demonically inspired false religion that has manifested in a myriad of ways, but all for the same purpose—to obscure the gospel and prevent people from worshipping the one true God. Even more, I hope this work has testified that as real as the powers behind nationalism are, the power of God in Christ is infinitely greater.

The January 6, 2021 Capitol Riot may be seen as an apocalyptic moment in the sense that it dramatically unveiled something true about the nature of our world. It revealed that the demonic idolatry of nationalism is a force that is alive and active, not just in the United States, but around the globe. But as providence would have it, January 6 is also a feast day on the Christian liturgical calendar. It is a day known as "The Epiphany," which celebrates the manifestation of the light of Christ to the gentiles.

So, despite nationalism's powerful and prominent force within this world, I pray this work has displayed how Christ has defeated the spiritual powers that fuel the rage of nations and has made a way for gentile people—people like me—to be included in the covenant community of God's people. As the Prophet Isaiah once sang in hope, "Arise, shine, for your light has come, and the glory of the LORD has risen upon you. For behold, darkness shall cover the earth, and thick darkness the peoples; but the LORD will arise upon you, and his glory will be seen upon you. And nations

shall come to your light, and kings to the brightness of your rising"
(Isa 60:1–3).

The nations will always rage until the day they kneel in homage to the Son and take refuge in him alone (Ps 2:12). With the Spirit and the Bride, I pray that this day would come quickly. Even so, come, Lord Jesus.

Bibliography

Acolatse, Esther E. *Powers, Principalities, and Spirits: Biblical Realism in Africa and the West.* Grand Rapids, MI: Eerdmans, 2018.

Allison, Gregg R. Allison. *Historical Theology.* Grand Rapids, MI: Zondervan, 2011.

Anderson, Benedict. *Imagined Communities: Reflections on the Origin and Spread of Nationalism.* Rev. ed. London: Verso, 2016.

Arnold, Bill T., and Bryan E. Beyer, eds. *Readings from the Ancient Near East.* Grand Rapids, MI: Baker Academic, 2002.

Arnold, Clinton E. *Magic and Power: The Concept of Power in Ephesians.* Eugene, OR: Wipf & Stock, 1989.

———. *Powers of Darkness: Principalities and Powers in Paul's Letters.* Downers Grove, IL: IVP Academic, 1992.

Augustine of Hippo. *St. Augustin's City of God and Christian Doctrine.* Edited by Philip Schaff. Translated by Marcus Dods. Buffalo, NY: Christian Literature, 1887.

Baldwin, Joyce G. *Daniel: An Introduction and Commentary.* Downers Grove, IL: InterVarsity, 1978.

Barclay, John M. G., and Simon J. Gathercole, eds. *Divine and Human Agency in Paul and His Cultural Environment.* New York: T. & T. Clark, 2008.

Basil of Caesarea. *St. Basil: Letters and Select Works.* Edited by Philip Schaff and Henry Wace. Translated by Blomfield Jackson. New York: Christian Literature, 1895.

Benoit, Pierre. "Pauline Angelology and Demonology: Reflexions on Designations of Heavenly Powers and on Origin of Angelic Evil According to Paul." *Religious Studies Bulletin* 3.1 (January 1983) 1–18.

Berkhof, Hendrik. *Christ and the Powers.* Translated by John H. Yoder. Scottdale, PA: Herald, 1977.

Berkhof, L. *Systematic Theology.* Grand Rapids, MI: Eerdmans, 1938.

Best, Ernest. *A Critical and Exegetical Commentary on Ephesians.* Edinburgh: T. & T. Clark International, 1998.

Block, Daniel I. *The Gods of the Nations: Studies in Ancient Near Eastern National Theology.* 2nd Ed. Eugene, OR: Wipf & Stock, 1988.

———. *Judges, Ruth.* Nashville: Broadman & Holman, 1999.

Bibliography

Boyd, Gregory A. *God at War: The Bible & Spiritual Conflict.* Downers Grove, IL: InterVarsity, 1997

Bruce, F. F. *The Epistles to the Colossians, to Philemon, and to the Ephesians.* Grand Rapids, MI: Eerdmans, 1984.

Bultmann, Rudolf. *New Testament and Mythology and Other Basic Writings.* Edited and translated by Schubert M. Ogden. Philadelphia: Fortress, 1984.

Caird, G. B. *Principalities and Powers: A Study in Pauline Theology, The Chancellor's Lectures for 1954 at Queens University.* Eugene, OR: Wipf & Stock, 2003.

Calvin, John. *Commentary on the Book of the Prophet Daniel.* Translated by Thomas Myers. Bellingham, WA: Logos, 2010.

——— . *Institutes of the Christian Religion.* Edited by John T. McNeill. Translated by Ford Lewis Battles. Louisville, KY: Westminster John Knox, 2011.

Charles, Robert Henry, ed. *Pseudepigrapha of the Old Testament.* Oxford: Clarendon, 1913.

Childs, Brevard S. *Isaiah.* The Old Testament Library. Louisville, KY: Westminster John Knox, 2001.

Collins, John Joseph, and Adela Yarbro Collins. *Daniel: A Commentary on the Book of Daniel.* Minneapolis: Fortress, 1993.

Comblin, José. *The Church and the National Security State.* Maryknoll, NY: Orbis, 1979.

Croasmun, Matthew. *The Emergence of Sin: The Cosmic Tyrant in Romans.* New York: Oxford University Press, 2017.

Cundall, Arthur E., and Leon Morris. *Judges and Ruth: An Introduction and Commentary.* Downers Grove, IL: InterVarsity, 1968.

Cuoto e Silva, Golbery. *Geopolítica do Brasil.* Rio de Janiero: José Olympio, 1967.

Darko, Daniel K. *Against Powers and Principalities: Spiritual Beings in Relation to Communal Identity and the Moral Discourse of Ephesians.* Plateau State, Nigeria: Hippo, 2020.

Dowley, Tim, ed. *Introduction to the History of Christianity.* Rev. ed. Minneapolis, MN: Fortress, 2002.

Evans, Craig A. "Inaugurating the Kingdom of God and Defeating the Kingdom of Satan." *Bulletin for Biblical Research* 15.1 (2005) 49–75.

Forbes, Christopher. "Pauline Demonology and/or Cosmology? Principalities, Powers and the Elements of the World in Their Hellenistic Context." *Journal for the Study of the New Testament* 24.3 (March 2002) 51–73.

Frame, John M. *The Doctrine of the Christian Life.* Phillipsburg, NJ: P&R, 2008.

Frankfurt, Henri. *Kingship and the Gods: A Study in Ancient Near Eastern Religion as the Integration of Society and Nature.* Chicago: University of Chicago Press, 1948.

Garland, David E. *2 Corinthians.* Nashville: Broadman & Holman, 1999.

Gat, Azar, with Alexander Yakobson. *Nations: The Long History and Deep Roots of Political Ethnicity and Nationalism.* New York: Cambridge University Press, 2013.

Gaventa, Beverly Roberts. "The Cosmic Power of Sin in Paul's Letter to the Romans: Toward a Widescreen Edition." *Interpretation* 58.3 (2004) 229–40.

Gorski, Philip S. and Samuel L. Perry. *The Flag and the Cross: White Christian Nationalism and the Threat to American Democracy.* Oxford: Oxford University Press, 2022.

Greidanus, Sidney. *Preaching Christ from Genesis: Foundations for Expository Sermons.* Grand Rapids, MI: Eerdmans, 2007.

Grosby, Steven. *Biblical Ideas of Nationality Ancient and Modern.* Winona Lake, IN: Eisenbrauns, 2012.

——— . *Nationalism: A Very Short Introduction.* Oxford: Oxford University Press, 2005.

Hastings, Adrian. *The Construction of Nationhood: Ethnicity, Religion, and Nationalism.* Cambridge: Cambridge University Press, 1997.

Hayes, Carlton J.H. *Nationalism: A Religion.* New York: Macmillan, 1960.

Hazony, Yoram. *The Virtue of Nationalism.* New York: Basic, 2018.

Heine, Ronald E. *Classical Christian Doctrine: Introducing the Essentials of the Ancient Faith.* Grand Rapids, MI: Baker Academic, 2013.

Heiser, Michael S. *Demons: What the Bible Really Says About the Powers of Darkness.* Bellingham, WA: Lexham, 2020.

——— . "Deuteronomy 32:8 and the Sons of God." *Bibliotheca Sacra* 158.629 (2001) 52–74.

——— . *The Unseen Realm: Recovering the Supernatural Worldview of the Bible.* Bellingham, WA: Lexham, 2015.

Higham, John "Indian Princess and Roman Goddess: The First Female Symbols of America." *Proceedings of the American Antiquarian Society* 100.1 (April 1990) 45–79.

Historic Creeds and Confessions. Electronic ed. Oak Harbor: Lexham Press, 1997.

Hobsbawm, E.J. *Nations and Nationalism since 1780: Programme, Myth, Reality.* 2nd ed. Cambridge, UK: Cambridge University Press, 1990.

Holland, Tom. *Contours of Pauline Theology: A Radical New Survey of the Influences on Paul's Biblical Writings.* Geanies House, Fearn, Ross-shire, Scotland: Mentor, 2004.

Horton, Michael Scott, ed. *Power Religion: The Selling Out of the Evangelical Church?* Chicago: Moody, 1992.

Hossfeld, Frank-Lothar, and Erich Zenger. *Psalms 2: A Commentary on Psalms 51–100.* Edited by Klaus Baltzer. Translated by Linda M. Maloney. Minneapolis, MN: Fortress, 2005.

Howard, David M., Jr. *Joshua.* Nashville: Broadman & Holman, 1998.

Hughes, R. Kent. *Acts: The Church Afire.* Wheaton, IL: Crossway, 1996.

Hutchinson, John and Anthony D. Smith, eds. *Nationalism.* Oxford: Oxford University Press, 1994.

Jenkins, Philip. *The Next Christendom: The Coming of Global Christianity.* Rev. ed. New York: Oxford University Press, 2007.

Justin Martyr. "The Second Apology of Justin." In *The Apostolic Fathers with Justin Martyr and Irenaeus,* edited by Alexander Roberts, James Donaldson, and A. Cleveland Coxe, 188–93. Buffalo, NY: Christian Literature, 1885.

Kawai, Kazuo. "The Divinity of the Japanese Emperor." *Political Science* 10.2 (1958) 3–14.

Keller, Timothy. *Counterfeit Gods: The Empty, Promises of Money, Sex, and Power, and the Only Hope That Matters.* New York: Dutton, 2009.

Kidd, Reggie M. "Ephesians: Power and Magic: The Concept of Power in Ephesians in Light of Its Historical Setting." *The Westminster Theological Journal* 56.1 (1994) 201–3.

Kidner, Derek. *Psalms 73–150: An Introduction and Commentary.* Downers Grove, IL: InterVarsity, 1975.

Koyzis, David T. *Political Visions and Illusions: A Survey and Critique of Contemporary Ideologies.* 2nd ed. Downers Grove, IL: IVP Academic, 2019.

Kraus, Hans-Joachim. *A Continental Commentary: Psalms 1–59.* Minneapolis, MN: Fortress, 1993.

Kreitzer, L Joseph. "Apotheosis of the Roman Emperor." *The Biblical Archaeologist* 53.4 (1990) 211–17.

Kruger, Michael J., ed. *A Biblical-Theological Introduction to the New Testament: The Gospel Realized.* Wheaton, IL: Crossway, 2016.

Kwon, Duke L. and Gregory Thompson. *Reparations: A Christian Call for Repentance and Repair.* Grand Rapids, MI: Brazos, 2021.

Ladd, George Eldon. *A Theology of the New Testament.* Grand Rapids, MI: Eerdmans, 1974.

Leithart, Peter J. *Between Babel and Beast: America and Empires in Biblical Perspective.* Eugene, OR: Cascade, 2012.

——— . *Delivered from the Elements of the World: Atonement, Justification, Mission.* Downers Grove, IL: IVP Academic, 2016.

Lewis, C.S. *God in the Dock: Essays on Theology and Ethics.* Edited by Walter Hooper. Grand Rapids, MI: Eerdmans, 1970.

——— . *The Screwtape Letters.* New York: HarperCollins, 1942.

——— . *The Weight of Glory: And Other Addresses.* HarperCollins, 1949.

Lowry, Rich. *The Case for Nationalism: How It Made Us Powerful, United, and Free.* New York: Broadside, 2019.

Luther, Martin. *Small Catechism.* St. Louis: Concordia, 1943.

Lyly, John. *Complete Works.* Oxford: Oxford University Press, 1902.

Marshall, I. Howard. *Acts: An Introduction and Commentary.* Downers Grove, IL: InterVarsity, 1980.

Martyn, J. Louis. *Galatians: A New Translation with Introduction and Commentary.* New Haven, CT: Yale University Press, 2000.

Mathews, K. A. *Genesis 1–11:26*. Nashville: Broadman & Holman, 1996.

Micheli, Jason. "Theology." *Christian Century* 136.11 (May 22, 2019) 26–27.

Miller, Stephen R. *Daniel*. Nashville: Broadman & Holman, 1994.

Moo, Douglas J. *The Epistle to the Romans*. Grand Rapids, MI: Eerdmans, 1996.

Mouw, Richard J. *When the Kings Come Marching In: Isaiah and the New Jerusalem*. Rev. ed. Grand Rapids, MI: Eerdmans, 2002.

O'Brien, Peter Thomas. *The Epistle to the Philippians: A Commentary on the Greek Text*. Grand Rapids, MI: Eerdmans, 1991.

Olson, Daniel C. "1 Enoch." In *Eerdmans Commentary on the Bible*, edited by James D. G. Dunn and John W. Rogerson, 904–41. Grand Rapids, MI: Eerdmans, 2003.

Orwell, George. *Notes on Nationalism*. London: Penguin, 2018.

Oswalt, John N. *The Book of Isaiah: Chapters 1–39*. Grand Rapids, MI: Eerdmans, 1986.

Pate, C. Marvin. "Revelation 2–19 and the Roman Imperial Cult." *Criswell Theological Review* 17.1 (Fall 2019) 67–82.

Plato, *The Dialogues of Plato*, Translated by B. Jowett. 3rd ed. Oxford: Clarendon, 1892.

Poythress, Vern S. "Territorial Spirits: Some Biblical Perspectives." *Urban Mission* 13 (December 1995) 37–49.

Radner, Karen. *Ancient Assyria: A Very Short Introduction*. Oxford: Oxford University Press, 2015.

Renan, Ernest. *Qu'est-ce qu'une nation?* Translated by Ida Mae Snyder. Paris: Calmann-Levy, 1882.

Reno, R.R. *The Return of the Strong Gods: Nationalism, Populism, and the Future of the West*. Washington, DC: Regenery Gateway, 2019.

Ridderbos, Herman. *Paul: An Outline of His Theology*. Grand Rapids, MI: Eerdmans, 1975.

Russell, D.S. *The Method and Message of the Jewish Apocalyptic: 200 BC–AD 100*. Philadelphia: Westminster, 1964.

Rutledge, Fleming. *The Crucifixion: Understanding the Death of Jesus*. Grand Rapids, MI: Eerdmans, 2015.

Seton-Watson, Hugh. *Nations and States: An Inquiry into the Origins of Nations and the Politics of Nationalism*. Boulder, CO: Westview, 1977.

Shellnutt, Kate. "China Tells Christians to Replace Images of Jesus with Communist President: Propaganda Effort in Poor Province Latest Sign of Xi Jinping Consolidating Control." *Christianity Today*, November 17, 2017.

Smith, Anthony D. *Chosen Peoples: Sacred Sources of National Identity*. New York: Oxford University Press, 2003.

———. *Nationalism: Theory, Ideology, History*. 2nd ed. Cambridge: Polity, 2013.

Smith, James K.A. *Cultural Liturgies*. Vol. 1, *Desiring the Kingdom: Worship, Worldview, and Cultural Formation*. Grand Rapids, MI: Baker Academic, 2009.

Spencer, Aìda BesanÁon. *2 Timothy and Titus: A New Covenant Commentary.* Eugene, OR: Cascade, 2014.

Steinbeck, John. *The Grapes of Wrath.* New York: Penguin, 1939.

Storrar, William. "'Vertigo' or 'Imago'? Nations in the Divine Economy." *Themelios* 21.3 (1996) 4–8.

Stott, John R. W. *God's New Society: The Message of Ephesians.* Downers Grove, IL: InterVarsity, 1979.

Thiselton, Anthony C. *The First Epistle to the Corinthians: A Commentary on the Greek Text.* Grand Rapids, MI: Eerdmans, 2000.

Tigay, Jeffrey H. *Deuteronomy.* Philadelphia: The Jewish Publication Society, 1996.

Tisby, Jemar. *The Color of Compromise: The Truth about the American Church's Complicity in Racism.* Grand Rapids, MI: Zondervan, 2019.

Towner, Philip H. *The Letters to Timothy and Titus.* Grand Rapids, MI: Eerdmans, 2006.

Waltke, Bruce K., and Cathi J. Fredricks. *Genesis: A Commentary.* Grand Rapids, MI: Zondervan, 2001.

Walton, John H., and J. Harvey Walton. *Demons and Spirits in Biblical Theology: Reading the Biblical Text in Its Cultural and Literary Context.* Eugene, OR: Cascade, 2019.

Whitehead, Andrew and Samuel L. Perry. *Taking America Back for God: Christian Nationalism in the United States.* New York: Oxford University Press, 2020.

Williams, Michael J. *The Prophet and His Message: Reading Old Testament Prophecy Today.* Phillipsburg, NJ: P&R, 2003.

Wink, Walter. *Engaging the Powers: Discernment and Resistance in a World of Domination.* Minneapolis, MN: Fortress, 1992.

——— . *Naming the Powers: The Language of Power in the New Testament.* Minneapolis, MN: Fortress, 1984.

——— . *The Powers That Be: Theology for a New Millennium.* New York: Doubleday, 1998.

——— . *Unmasking the Powers: The Invisible Powers that Determine Human Existence.* Minneapolis, MN: Fortress, 1986.

Wylie-Kellerman, Bill. *Principalities in Particular: A Practical Theology of the Powers That Be.* Minneapolis, MN: Fortress, 2017.

Young, Edward J. *Daniel.* Carlisle, PA: Banner of Truth, 1949.

Zhao, Dingxin. "The Mandate of Heaven and Performance Legitimization in Historical and Contemporary China." *American Behavioral Scientist* 53.3 (November 2009) 416–33.